SEARCHING FOR JOHN DEWITT

How 80 Forgotten Letters from the Trenches of WWI Revealed Timeless Lessons of Honor and Courage

John Chase, MD

Published by Hellgate Press
(An imprint of L&R Publishing, LLC)
2305 Ashland St., #104-176
Ashland, OR 97520
email: sales@hellgatepress.com

Editor: Harley B. Patrick
Book design: Michael Campbell
Cover design: Grant Guidry

ISBN:978-1-954163-93-5

Printed and bound in the United States of America
First edition 10 9 8 7 6 5 4 3 2 1

Searching for

JOHN DEWITT

How 80 Forgotten Letters from the Trenches of WWI Revealed Timeless Lessons of Honor and Courage

JOHN CHASE, MD

To John Ryder DeWitt

To members of the military,
the quiet patriots who do their jobs without
chest pounding or self-congratulation

And to former military, the modest heroes
who came home and moved on
with little fanfare

I hope this book will encourage families
to ask their veteran relatives about their
military service and not have to learn about
it by reading long-lost letters 100 years later.

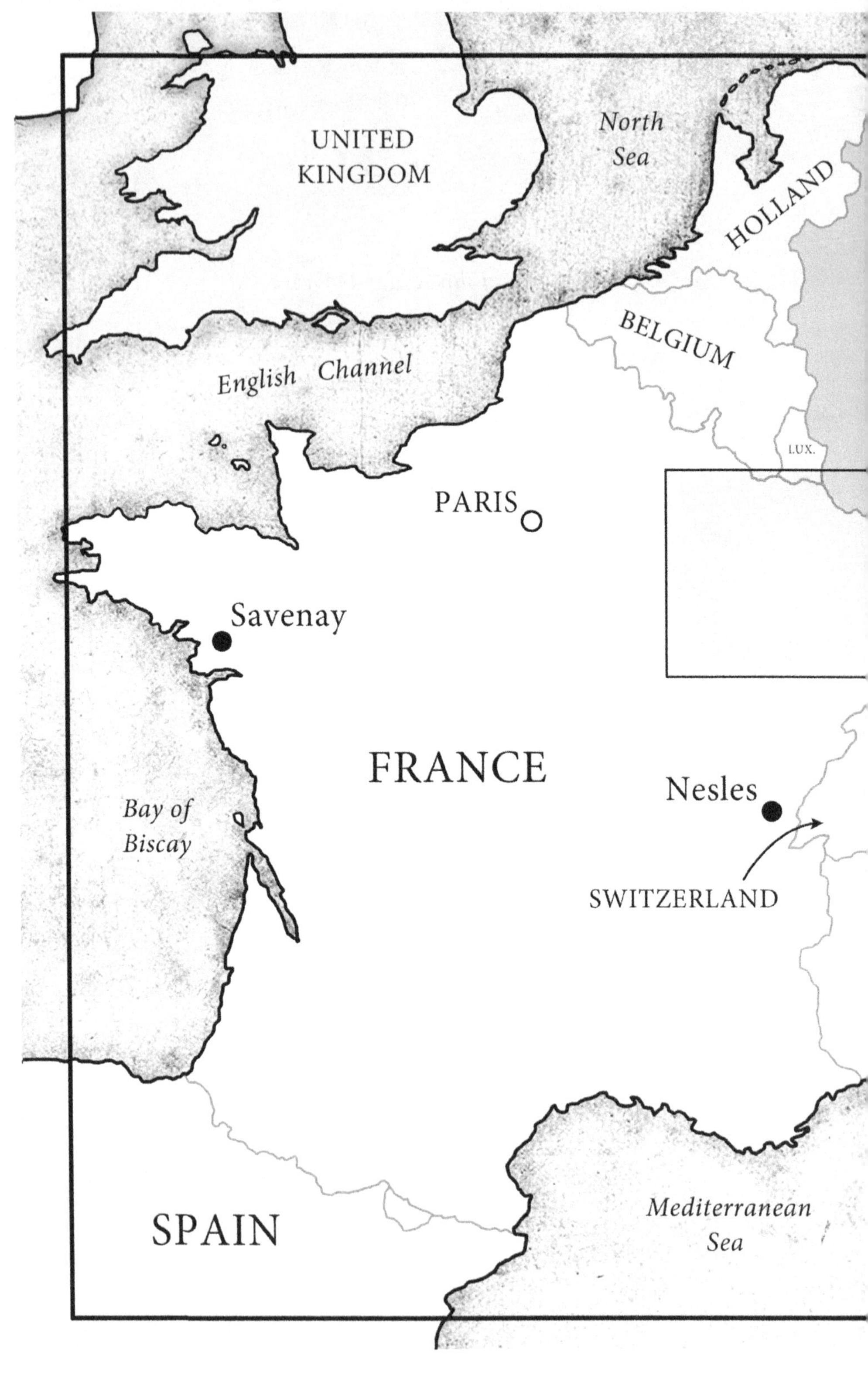
UNITED
KINGDOM
North
Sea
HOLLAND
BELGIUM
English Channel
LUX.
PARIS
Savenay
FRANCE
Nesles
Bay of
Biscay
SWITZERLAND
SPAIN
Mediterranean
Sea

GERMANY
John DeWitt's movements in France
November 1917 to November 1918
Suippes
FRANCE
Luneville
Vancouleurs
Baccarat
Rimacourt
Badonviller
ITALY
Adriatic Sea

1

PROLOGUE

AN UNEXPECTED CALL from my sister Abby more than a century after Billy Schupp died unnerved me at first. She had found a cache of letters written by our grandfather, John DeWitt, that had sat for years in shoeboxes in our uncle's garage, unread.

Those letters would send me on a journey I had not packed for nor planned to make.

Neatly written by our grandfather, the letters were unfailingly cheerful and reassuring. They would open for me a chapter of John DeWitt's life I knew nothing about.

My unassuming grandfather, it seemed, was a war hero.

His letters home left much unsaid about what he was going through. The fact that he packed them away when he returned home and never spoke of his experiences was perhaps his most profound statement of all.

I resolved to find out what he had gone through and why he had kept quiet about it.

I was not prepared for what I would discover.

My first clue came from a story about two trench runners from Iowa, both serving with the 168th Infantry in France.

BILLY SCHUPP, a young runner with the American Expeditionary Force from Iowa, died in western France in July 1918. What remained of his body after the fragments of a German shell ripped through him as he sprinted near the front lines was thrown violently upward in an explosion of mud and chaos.

Two hundred yards behind him, Al Boysen, his good friend and fellow Iowan, watched helplessly.

Billy Schupp's violent demise was not an isolated event. He was one of 125,000 Allied soldiers killed or wounded that month during the Battle of the Soissonnais and the Ourcq.

The German army was on the move in what would be a last desperate offensive to regain its supply routes in western France. For two hellish weeks, Allied Forces would throw all they had at the attacking Germans. As their comrades waited with bayonets fixed, anticipating a German assault, young men like Billy Schupp and Al Boysen had another crucial job to do, deliver messages that would prevent the American lines from being overrun.

Boysen and Schupp were vital cogs in the effort to stop the Germans. They were also expendable.

Schupp and Boysen, good friends from Council Bluffs, were members of the 168th Regiment, part of the famed Rainbow Division that had arrived in France six months earlier. Rainbow Division volunteers included the poet Joyce Kilmer and future Word War II spymaster William "Wild Bill" O'Donovan. The Rainbow Division's chief of staff was an ambitious young officer on the rise by the name of Douglas McArthur.

Schupp and Boysen were trench runners, members of an elite group whose mortality more often than not was counted in days. They had been chosen by unit commanders who recognized their athleticism and quick minds, assets in perhaps the most thankless job on the Western Front. Schupp and Boysen were among tens of thousands of young American men, some barely old enough to shave, who had volunteered to fight the Germans thousands of miles from their homes in New York and Nebraska and Ohio and Arkansas, every one of the forty-eight states, Arizona having joined the Union only six years before, when Schupp and Boysen were adolescents.

Schupp and Boysen knew their life expectancies were tenuous at best. They understood their deaths would not be a matter of bad luck but the expected outcome of soldiers delivering messages through the muck and mazes of deeply dug trenches and the open spaces between the lines—a maelstrom of falling shells, thick crossfire, and anxious and accurate German snipers.

Billy Schupp's brutal death was not an anomaly. It was a daily and predictable ending for trench runners.

Schupp and Boysen began their training at Camp Dodge, just outside Des Moines. They were among 115,000 Iowans to enlist after President Woodrow Wilson asked Congress to declare war on Germany on April 9, 1917.

They continued their training at Camp Mills, on Long Island, a raucous and hastily expanding training ground of some 40,000 men on their way to war in France. Just ten miles outside New York City, Camp Mills was larger than either Council Bluffs or Des Moines. Earlier that year, New York City had seen angry rioters take to the streets to protest rising costs of food prompted by the war they were about to enter.

That was not their concern.

On rare occasions when they were not training, Schupp and Boysen went to the movies, and marched in a parade as visiting Iowa Governor William Harding watched from the reviewing stand. They played basketball, went to church on Sunday. They visited Coney Island, whose rides included a three-story carousel called the El Dorado and rode its famed Ocean Roller Coaster. They walked the beach at Rockaway. They lapped up the city crowds and excitement and adoration.

These were all pleasant diversions, amusing interludes before the storm.

Mostly, though, they trained. They were headed to France to fight.

Schupp and Boysen boarded the S.S. *President Grant* along with the rest of the 168th, some 10,000 men, and headed to Europe. The *Grant's* captain and officers were no doubt wary of lethal German submarines. It was after all, a German submarine attack on the *Lusitania* off Kinsale, Ireland, that had eventually brought America into the war.

The soldiers packed aboard the *Grant* had other things on their minds. They were about to do their part in what they considered a noble cause.

By December 1917, the lives of Schupp and Boysen and the other men of the 168th Regiment had changed dramatically. All the training and drills and exertions they had invested in had not properly prepared them for what awaited. No training could possibly recreate the sordidness and desperation of life in the trenches or the daily bombardments and death.

War on the Western Front, enemies within shouting distance, was barely controlled chaos, an imprecise and ineffective attempt of at least the appearance of order and strategy when all around was bedlam.

At it very center, the most essential of all elements, was the ability to communicate to other Allies along the front about where one was and what one was planning to do.

With imperfect technology and the constant destruction of fragile radio and rudimentary telephone lines, communication between trapped command posts, where coordination was critical to moving forward, depended on the legs of runners like Schupp and Boysen.

I would learn much later, they would depend on my grandfather's legs too.

By July, the once-raw recruits were physically fit, hardened emotionally, and certainly fatalistic. By then they had seen death up close. By then their minds were able to quickly process where they were and how to get anywhere else in a landscape that changed constantly. Knowing the lay of the land was not simply an admirable talent for runners, it was a matter of life and death. Map reading, speed, and precision were essential skills for a trench runner.

So was courage.

By July they had grown used to the drill. They knew at some point they would be chosen from the pool of company runners to deliver a message in what became a macabre lottery. It was the luck of the draw. They did not mind. That was what they had agreed to do, and they would do it. Everyone in the pool of runners understood the odds and played the game.

In July, as the battle raged around them, Schupp and Boysen's number came up. It was their turn and they walked quickly to the company command post, a weakly undescriptive term for what was nothing more than a dark dugout trench. Wearing the red arm band that announced their specialty, a mark of honor that also served as a perfect target for snipers, Schupp and Boysen stood in front of the company commander and performed a ritual they had done many times before.

He needed a message delivered to battalion headquarters dug into the open field ahead of them, a once pastoral landscape of gentle hills and groves of trees.

Their commander handed them a message on paper, which they memorized. Paper and the message it contained could easily be pulled from the pocket of a dead runner by the Germans.

Once both men read the message, they returned the piece of paper to the commander. Then they recited it aloud. The Germans could not pirate a message from a dead man.

Schupp left first. Boysen followed 200 yards behind, German artillery pounding the area.

Boysen watched as his good friend was hit, Schupp's body tossed in the air by the explosion. Remnants of the exploding shell that killed Schupp struck Boysen's legs, nearly bringing him down.

He had no doubt Schupp was dead.

Bleeding and ashen, he continued to the command post and delivered the message.

Then he turned to head back to his friend.

Two others in the command post grabbed his shoulders and pulled him back.

"Where are you going?" they asked.

"Where am I going?" Boysen replied, anguished.

"I'm going back to get my buddy."

Then he fainted.

JOHN DEWITT served with Billy Schupp and Al Boysen. All three were from Council Bluffs. He had trained with them at Camp Dodge and Camp Mills. He wore the red arm band, made his own frantic runs and delivered the same crucial messages and took part in the same daily lottery.

His letters home, found in a box more than a century later, made little mention of such things.

I resolved to learn why.

ONE

I DON'T REMEMBER asking the question.

When my grandfather's answer came forty years later, long after he died, I was shaken.

It began with a call from my sister Abby in May 2020.

She had been helping our eighty-year-old Uncle Jack move from his large house in Oklahoma City to an assisted living near her home in Lincoln, Nebraska. Rifling through his cluttered garage she had found several shoeboxes containing some old letters.

"What are these Jack?"

"Oh, just some old letters my Dad wrote to his parents in Council Bluffs when he was in World War I."

Jack had retired after a long career with the FBI. His father's war exploits apparently had not interested him, and no doubt, his father had rarely spoken of them.

Abby was intrigued.

They seemed to be much more than "some old letters."

She began skimming and two things jumped out immediately. After years sitting unprotected in shoeboxes in Jack's Oklahoma City garage, they were remarkably well preserved. Even though all were posted hurriedly from the summer of 1917 to the fall of 1918 as our grandfather John DeWitt made his way through training camps in Iowa and New York to Europe, they were written with beautiful, flawless penmanship.

"What did he do in the war, Jack?"

"Oh, he was a runner in the trenches," Jack said, adding nothing more.

After moving Jack to his new and more manageable apartment, she brought the letters back to her home in Lincoln and called me about her find.

I was intrigued by the discovery but not overly excited. The country was reeling from Covid and I was not enthusiastic about getting on an airplane. Old letters from our grandfather seemed interesting, but not enough to drop everything.

I made a trip to read them in August, traveling to Lincoln after I had made to trip to see my ailing father in Arkansas.

Abby and I sorted the letters, close to eighty, and put them in chronological order. As we sat at her dining room table, Abby told me she had learned our grandfather had won a Purple heart, had run the trenches, and had been gassed and hospitalized.

I perked up a bit.

Grampa, as we called him, had never mentioned this. Still, I was not overwhelmed with curiosity. It seemed an interesting part of family lore, but nothing more.

I read through the letters quickly that afternoon. All were upbeat, optimistic, and seemed to me nothing more than an interesting part of my grandfather's life I had never heard about, a bit of family history tucked away for years in shoeboxes.

My perspective would change dramatically.

A few hours later, the quiet and unassuming John Ryder DeWitt, who had died years before, would answer the question I don't recall asking.

I was floored.

Abby and I began opening other boxes from Jack DeWitt's old house. In one marked "FBI files" I found a typewritten note my grandfather had, in 1972, dictated to his secretary in the one-man law office he ran in Griswold, Iowa, for years after he returned from France. The note was written to me and Jack DeWitt.

As I read the note, I saw my bow-tied grandfather sitting behind his wide oak desk. I could almost smell the comforting aroma of his cigars forty years later.

I sat upright, suddenly awake.

John DeWitt would die a year later from colon cancer. Did he know that he was sick? Was that what prompted him to finally open up about his war experiences?

October 17, 1972

To: Jack DeWitt, John Chase and any other interested persons

You have asked me about my war experiences.

I told you I was a Battalion runner, but I don't think it meant a great deal to you.

I recalled that there was an article in the Stars and Stripes about runners.

The other day Joel Boone brought in a book containing articles of the Stars and Stripes.

I looked and found the above account.

Al Boysen and Billy Schupp were members of my own Company L.

They were company runners.

I was located at battalion headquarters.

Each company had two runners there.

It was after the above-described battle that I was recommended for a DFC (but it should have been DSC-Distinguished Service Cross)

I was given a Division citation rather than the DSC.

I thought you would be interested in reading same.

"Holy crap," I said to Abby.

I was jarred and suddenly awake, startled, wondering who Billy Schupp and Al Boysen were.

With the note was a yellowing and fragile newspaper clipping from T*he Star and Stripes* that recounted Billy Schupp's death in France, dated Friday, August 9, 1918, with the headline:

SPEEDY RUNNERS NORTH OF OURCQ RACE WITH DEATH

Wearers of the Red Brassard Carry Tiding of Battle as Hun Goes Back

Men Cross Fire-Swept Areas With Messages That Mean Defeat or Victory for Comrades

They were young and slim and could run like the wind. They were together on the greatest day and hour of their lives. It came on the historic fortnight of July 1918, for their regimens was one that waited with fixed bayonets when the mighty German offensive broke like the surf against the expectant Allied line and did not sit down till the Marne and the Ourcq lay behind them.

It was apparent John DeWitt had had a radically different life in the army than the one he recounted so cheerfully in his letters to his mother.

Until that day in Lincoln, I had never seen my grandfather's note. I had not seen or read the article. I don't recall any curiosity on my part about his time in Europe in 1917 and 1918, and I can't remember asking about it.

My grandfather was correct about my lack of interest in 1972. I was eighteen years old when he dictated the note, a self-absorbed Iowa high school senior with other things on my mind—graduation, the football season I was in the middle of, what lay ahead for college.

His experiences in World War I would not have meant that much to me then. I doubt I would have done anything to learn more.

Reading the note in 2020, I felt he was reaching out to me from the grave!

The note and the *Stars and Stripes* article were the beginning pieces of a puzzle I'd try to assemble over the next few years.

I wanted to learn as much as I could about what exactly John DeWitt had gone through and why he had closed the door on his experiences when he returned to Iowa.

Growing up, he was simply Grampa, a man I'd watch football with when we visited his home in Griswold. Our conversations, as many conversations between a boy and his soft-spoken grandfather, were always pleasant but superficial.

Reading the note and the article in 2020 chilled me and sparked my curiosity.

I reread *The Stars and Stripes* article, and something else caught my attention.

> *Go to anyone who any day or week of the battle where it was hottest and ask who were its heroes. He will want to name all the men who put their shoulders to its*

> *tremendous burden, from ammunitions drivers, plowing stubbornly on through maddening miles of mud, knowing and asking no sleep for many days and nights, to the battalion commanders, who could not and would not remember what the books said about their place being behind the line. But if he must single out one group for tribute, the chances are he will reluctantly pass the others by and say: "The Runners."*

What had John DeWitt done during the war, and why had he never talked about it?

I wanted to know more.

I thought back to the pleasant but distant man I had known and visited over the years from our home in Ida Grove, two hours north of Griswold, on holidays. I remembered his big belly and cigars and voracious appetite.

I thought of the times he'd take my father to play golf at the Atlantic Country Club and how we'd get to swim in the club pool while they were on the course. I remembered him taking me to his law office and walking up the long flight of stairs, exercise, he said, that would keep him healthy.

I remember trying to sleep through his raucous snoring in the bedroom next to his and Grandma's. Grandma snored too, but could not hold a candle to his racket, which seemed to rattle the windows.

We'd watch football together but said little.

Sitting in Lincoln, I reread the letters, all written to his mother, and noticed some clues to the young John DeWitt.

He was only weeks away from his twenty-first birthday when he began writing home, not much older than I was in 1972. His letters were much the same, pleasant, for the most part upbeat and optimistic, unfailingly cheerful.

I'd see he was a devout Catholic, often mentioning Mass and Confession. He was caring, unfailingly sending money from his slim paycheck home.

I would learn later he was making $30 a month for his efforts, the equivalent of about $550 today for putting his life on the line.

> *"Did you get the order for $10? I will try to make it $15 next pay day."*

I would notice he was hungry for news from home, his normal easy-going banter would grow more irritable when he failed to get a prompt reply. I'd see also he was eager for packages of cookies and doughnuts and clothing.

I'd see his kindness and empathy. He once wrote home suggesting a spinster neighbor, Miss Sprague, "adopt," a fellow soldier Harry O'Connor who seemed to have no family and thus no packages.

He was modest to a fault, only briefly mentioned being chosen as a runner—a rigorous and challenging review process I would learn later—and never revealing he had the most dangerous job in the Army.

He was capable of complaining, I'd learn.

> *Our tents are cold and it is windy and dusty so excuse the dirt. This really is the dirtiest camp that ever was. You can't keep clean and I take a shower every day and the water would be warm alongside of ice water and the wind is chilly too.*

Before the cigars I remember clearly, there were cigarettes, once writing home delightedly about a gift of a "a carton of Camels."

He was proud that he enlisted, and proud of his lack of fear.

My reading that afternoon was superficial. I wanted to know more.

There was much left unsaid in those letters.

In the middle of a war where his life was on the line, where his friends died with predictable violence every day, he wrote to his parents that all was well.

What was really going on?

I needed time with the letters, to study them, to research what was happening at the time he wrote them.

It took another two years to get them in front of me at home in Florida after other family members had shared them.

Once I did, my search for John DeWitt became focused. By the summer of 2022, I began in earnest, searching to learn as much as I could about of part of history that had long faded, of young American men who sacrificed everything.

John DeWitt had been a part of it, yet he was silent about it.

Now he was speaking directly to me.

I would learn during my later search to read between the lines of John DeWitt's letters.

I would discover what he went through, and why he could not explain Hell to his devoutly Catholic parents, or to anyone else when he returned to Iowa after the war—perhaps even to himself.

Certainly, it was not something he could explain to his grandson.

I resolved to learn as much as I could about John DeWitt and his comrades, what they fought for, and what they had gone through.

TWO

I HAD ONCE asked my grandfather what he had done in the war, but apparently, I did not have the time or inclination to listen. Finding his letters more than a century after he wrote them, I realized, was my chance to finally hear what he had to say.

John Ryder DeWitt was not a man to pat himself on the back or call attention to himself and share what he had gone through.

I took it on myself, his oldest grandson, to fill in the blanks. I would learn that army censors severely limited what he could write home. But I would also sense through his letters home that he was leaving clues—the dates on his letters home, the mention of a popular war correspondent's accounts of what was going on, hints at battles and where he was.

I had only to follow them.

Assembling the puzzle pieces of John Ryder DeWitt's life began tentatively.

As the family stories amassed, I learned John DeWitt was a proud man who did what he thought was right—in his work, with his family, and in his community. John DeWitt was a quiet patriot. He did not feel the need to raise his voice or beat his chest for doing what he thought was the right thing to do. He was not alone in silence. Many men returning from that war did the same.

Perhaps, I thought, I could speak for him, tell the story he once tried to tell me so many years before. Along the way, maybe I could tell the story of other men who fought and died in what many called, without irony, The War to End All Wars, who returned home and never spoke of it again.

I would try to learn the things he could not or would not tell his family.

His first letter home, in the summer of 1917, from his first posting at Iowa's Camp Dodge, captured his attitude. He was simply doing his job, concerned about his family, and getting things done.

> *Wednesday night*
>
> *Dearest Mother, Dad and the girls,*
>
> *Haven't heard from you in a day or so—what's wrong? Everything is just fine here, all okay and everything plenty work and very little time to write. Will have to make this short and sweet. We started to drill Monday and it's a drill too, believe me, our two weeks or so of ease sure softened me up.*
>
> *We got paid tonight and I am enclosing ten dollars. Hoping you can use the same. It is all that I can spare this time as I owed $10 already. Will try and do better next time but this ought to help. How are the girls getting along in school? Tell them to write. You ought to be able to send me a short note every day. It sure helps me to keep smiling, believe me.*
>
> *It is the same old story here, day in and day out. Went to church last Sunday, sure was nice. They have been giving us some new equipment today, belts and bayonets and first aid pack.*

> *Tell Dad that box was sure a lifesaver. I did a little washing today. It is getting late and I am sleepy so will have to close for a time. We took some pictures today at camp so when I get them, I will send you some. The water in the showers here are sure cold and all the same as ice.*
>
> *Give my regards to all and loads of love to all.*

My first steps in learning more about my grandfather were collecting faded memories, including my own. My search soon began to resemble a game of telephone, where each time a story was passed on it changed slightly, the lines between fact and family lore blurred.

As I started digging, I'd find an affectionate recounting of his life from a memoir my mother, John DeWitt's daughter, Maribeth, had written. I spoke with my Uncle Jack and collected anecdotes passed down through the years by people who had known him.

I pored over old family photos. In each he is always smiling benignly, even in a snapshot of him in bed, courtesy of the broken back he sustained in a car accident taken shortly before my parents' wedding. I took that constant, subtle smile as a sign of his persistence, of his unflappability.

As the puzzle began to take shape, I became certain that John DeWitt had lived a full life. He was a successful small-town attorney who dealt with estate work, wills, and contracts. One story I heard said he had once gotten a man off Death Row in his only jury trial, and that the man would send him a small gift each year on the anniversary of his freedom. He had a long marriage to my grandmother, Helen Brennan, a girl from Omaha he met after the war, with whom he had two children, my mother Maribeth, born in 1929, and Jack, born in 1938.

He was active in the Griswold community, and in state and national Republican campaigns, and was an avid supporter of Dwight D. Eisenhower, the former general who would become a two-term president. Politics engaged him, as did current events, and my mother would recount how he and Helen would listen to news on radio broadcasts from a station in Omaha daily. In 1955, he and my grandmother bought a television, the new medium they had sampled by joining other townsfolk watching at their friends, the Hokenstads.

He loved to play bridge and golf.

Throughout his life, family meant everything to him. He would write home during his time in the army without fail nearly every week, even in the heat of combat. He was an attentive father, doting on my mother and never missing a football game of Jack's.

He loved to eat—based on his letters home and my recollections of his wide belly, a lifetime affection.

He was a proud man, of his military service, of his Irishness, and of his Catholicism.

He was active in veterans' affairs, and he loved his cigars.

By the time I finished my search I would have a profound respect for my distant grandfather and a startling clarity about what he had gone through, and why he chose not to disinter the darker memories of his time in the army in 1917 and 1918. He buried those memories like had had buried so many of his comrades. Dwelling on the details would have no doubt unsettled the calm life he carved out for himself in Griswold.

I collected what I could about his comments on the war and used them as springboards to ferret out more information.

Jack could recall only two stories his father had told him about his time in the army. The passage over to Europe on a packed troopship from New York was rough, John DeWitt had recalled, and everyone was sick. vomiting their guts out over the rail.

Once in France, he told Jack, members of his 168th Infantry found themselves bivouacked next to French soldiers whose commissary sold wine. The entire American division was drunk for two days, my grandfather recounted to Jack.

When my mother was away at college, my grandfather would write her long typewritten pages in which he described his life, though there was little detail about his time in the war.

He wrote only in generalities to my mother. He had entered the service and became part of the Rainbow Division of 168th infantry of the US Army and was sent to France. He was a runner in the trenches, was awarded a Purple Heart for getting gassed by chemical weapons, and shot in the leg. To me, this only scratched the surface. He went no further in explaining to his daughter what the deadly job of runner entailed. I would find out.

My grandfather wrote my mother that after the war ended, he had won a coin toss and a berth home on an American-bound ship over a fellow soldier.

When he returned to Iowa, he helped form an American Legion post, a group in which he remained active for the rest of his life. But he would speak only in generalities about his service. He was proud enough of his contributions that in his last days, ill with colon cancer, he insisted on being treated in a Veterans' Hospital.

As I studied the letters he wrote home to his mother and family, I searched for clues about the twenty one-year-old

John DeWitt. He was forthright, usually cheerful and uncomplaining. I wanted to know more to understand why he fought and why he buried what he had gone through in France when he returned.

I knew I needed to know as much as I could to discover the John DeWitt I was unfamiliar with, the man outside the quiet Grampa I had known. Once I did I knew I could chart his path from Council Bluffs to France and learn as much as I could about what he had gone through as he was telling his parents not to worry.

Slowly, a picture began to gel.

The proud American soldier was the son of Canadian immigrants. His father, John R. DeWitt, was born in Perth County, Ontario, in 1862. His mother, Agnes Bridget Ryder, was born in St. Catherine's, Ontario in 1867. The couple were married in October 1892, in St. Paul, Minnesota.

A short piece in the *St. Paul Daily* Globe announced the wedding.

> *At the cathedral Tuesday morning, John DeWitt and Miss Agnes Ryder, sister of J. J. Ryder, were united in marriage by Rev. Dr. Heffron. The wedding was a quiet one, attended only by relatives and intimate friends of the contracting parties. The groom was kept in good countenance by his brother, Charles DeWitt. Miss Mary O'Malley was bridesmaid. The bride was handsomely gowned in gray, and carried a bridal bouquet of roses, while Miss O'Malley wore a pretty street costume. After the ceremony at the church the bridal party was driven to 622 Canada street, the future home of Mr. and Mrs. DeWitt. where relatives and friends congregated to enjoy a bountiful wedding repast. Mr. and Mrs. DeWitt left on the evening train for a trip to Chicago.*

My grandfather was born in St. Paul on August 30, 1896, the first of seven children. Three of his brothers would die in childhood. His three sisters—whom he would address in his letters home as "the girls"—Anne, Mary Clare, and Helen—were all born in Minneapolis.

The elder John DeWitt worked as a brakeman on the C.G. and W. railway, and when my grandfather was around ten years old, he moved the family 400 miles southwest from the Minneapolis St. Paul area to Council Bluffs. Iowa.

Council Bluffs was a major transportation hub.

It was likely a big change for my grandfather. The Minneapolis St. Paul area had a population of more than 200,000 at the time. Council Bluffs less than 30,000. Council Bluffs, on the banks of the Missouri River just across from Omaha, Nebraska, had long been the starting point for westward expeditions. The Mormon Trail had started there, and Lewis and Clarke had passed through. In 1869, the newly constructed transcontinental railroad was connected to rail lines from the eastern United States there.

As a young boy in Council Bluffs, John DeWitt got a job at a local firehouse caring for its horses. Even as an older adult in Griswold, he loved to follow fire engines.

In adulthood, Anne Rose, Mary Clare, and Helen would all move to New York City, returning once a year to Council Bluffs. I would hear scattered stories about their lives, about how they had left small-town life for the excitement of jobs working as executive secretaries for high-powered men in big firms in the big city.

Family lore recounts that the sisters, in the way that family stories can be frank, were, indelicately, less than attractive. Jack recounted that they were "homely." Another story said that Anne had been jilted and had never gotten over it. My grandfather, at five foot ten, was considered tall in those days and it appeared to be a family trait. His nickname for his sister Anne was "stretch."

John DeWitt's father would die in 1920, not long after my grandfather returned from France, and his wife, whom was called Nana, would move to New York to be with her daughters. Clare would die there in 1937 of tuberculosis.

In my search, I'd find two eerie coincidences that perhaps offered a sign of some genetic heritage from my grandfather. One story related that John DeWitt had longed to go to medical school but simply could not afford it. I would become an orthopaedic surgeon, my sister Abby, a registered nurse.

I'd also learn that my grandfather had affectionately called my mother "Millie"—the same name my daughter, with no inkling of my mother's nickname, had given her daughter.

In his letters to my mother, John DeWitt had said he became a traveling salesman, with a long route through Texas and Oklahoma, but his heart was not in it. With medical school out of the question, after he returned from France, he took advantage of the small funds available to returning veterans and enrolled in Creighton University Law School. He would take the Iowa State Bar Exam and pass without graduating.

Around that time, he would meet, court, and marry the woman we all knew as Grandma D, Helen Brennan, a city girl from Omaha, in 1927.

Helen Brennan DeWitt had attended Iowa State University where she was a member of Alpha Gamma Delta. Like her husband, she was active in the American Legion Auxiliary the Catholic Church Altar Society, and numerous bridge clubs. She was also a member of the Republican Party of

Iowa and represented the Party as a delegate to the National Convention in 1952.

Griswold at the time had a population of around 1,000, and family lore has it the confines of small-town life had been a bone of contention for Helen, the big city girl from Omaha.

There they would live out their lives, quite happily and contentedly.

In the summer of 2022, as I was just beginning my search for my grandfather at my father's funeral, I'd spoken with a couple who had been best friends of my parents, and who in their later years would often play bridge with my grandfather on visits back to Iowa.

At my father's funeral, Dick and Evelyn Teegen, now in their 90s, had driven from Minnesota to Arkansas to pay their respects, a telling tribute to their affection for my mother and father and our family. That included John DeWitt, who they were fond of.

Evelyn Teegen had graduated from Iowa State in 1953 and had gone on to become an influential Republican, serving as the national chair for the Minnesota delegation of the Republican National Committee. She had later been appointed by George H.W. Bush as ambassador to Fiji.

It was a bright moment. The Teegans were a vital connection to my grandfather's life and full of stories that made him come alive just as I was beginning my search.

I knew I had a long way to go, but I was heartened.

Then I recalled another thing that opened the door a bit more. In one of his long letters to my mother, my grandfather had written of his fondness for a poem, "In Flanders Fields," written by Canadian physician and soldier John McRae, who would die in the war.

I looked it up.

In Flanders fields the poppies blow
Between the crosses, row on row,
That mark our place; and in the sky
The larks, still bravely singing, fly
Scarce heard amid the guns below.

We are the Dead. Short days ago
We lived, felt dawn, saw sunset glow,
Loved and were loved, and now we lie,
In Flanders fields.

Take up our quarrel with the foe:
To you from failing hands we throw
The torch; be yours to hold it high.
If ye break faith with us who die
We shall not sleep, though poppies grow
In Flanders fields.

It chilled me. Perhaps McRae was speaking for my grandfather, saying the things he felt best to be left unsaid.

I had much to do to learn more.

And I would.

THREE

THE NEWS WAS impossible to ignore.

With commercial radio still four years away, the word spread in its usual fashion. Banner headlines in every newspaper in the country and its territories announced on April 6, 1917 that America was at war with Germany.

In the nation's capital, *The Washington Evening Star*'s boldface headline, U.S. AT WAR WITH GERMANY, was typical. *The Boston Journal's* announcement followed suit: U.S. ENTERS WORLD WAR. *The Daily Alaska Press*, blared the news more succinctly, WAR! In the Midwest, the Bemidji, Minnesota, *Daily Pioneer* ran STATE OF WAR IS DECLARED.

In Iowa, *The Atlantic News Telegraph* filled the top of its front page with UNITED STATES NOW AT WAR WITH GERMANY.

John Ryder DeWitt was caught in the fervor. For an ambitious twenty-year-old frustrated about his inability to afford medical school, drifting in a traveling sales job, he was no doubt electrified when he heard America was at war in Europe.

It gave him purpose beyond the small-city life he was living.

He wasted little time in volunteering to join the effort.

As the news spread, suspicion would mix with the patriotism the announcement aroused as the country began preparation to send troops to Europe.

Fearing the new medium of amateur radio would be misused by those sympathetic to the German cause, one of the government's first acts was to shut down or take control of an estimated 13,500 radio sets across the country, as what was seen as a passing fad grew. In San Jose, California, City Manager Thomas H. Reed, declared that "owning a wireless apparatus was an act of treason." In Buffalo, Erie County Sheriff Edward Stengel announced that "My deputies then will make a systematic search throughout the county for radio apparatus, no matter how big or small."

The tensions had been building for months.

Earlier that year, German submarines under orders from Kaiser Wilhelm II sank ten American merchant ships from February 3 through April 4, 1917. Americans were outraged.

In a speech before a special joint session of Congress, President Woodrow Wilson called for a resolution to join the war in Europe, then more than two years old. The fighting in Europe had been devastating, but the United States had maintained its neutrality. By April 1917, when America joined the effort, a million soldiers in the French army had been killed. In 1916's Battle of Verdun alone, the French lost about 160,000.

Wilson, who had long urged staying out of the war, told the Joint Session, "Armed neutrality is impracticable."

"The wrongs against which we now array ourselves," he said, "are no common wrongs; they cut to the very roots of human life."

Wilson made his point clearly.

"The present German submarine warfare against commerce is a warfare against mankind.

"There are, it may be, many months of fiery trial and sacrifice ahead of us. It is a fearful thing to lead this great peaceful people into war, into the most terrible and disastrous of all wars, civilization itself seeming to be in the balance. But the right is more precious than peace, and we shall fight for the things which we have always carried nearest our hearts—for democracy, for the right of those who submit to authority to have a voice in their own governments, for the rights and liberties of small nations, for a universal dominion of right by such a concert of free peoples as shall bring peace and safety to all nations and make the world itself at last free."

After several days of debate, Congress approved the resolution 373 to 50.

It would be the first time in American history its troops would fight on foreign soil.

With what I had learned of my grandfather and how he led his life, he did not equivocate about joining Wilson's call to action. For him, enlisting in the army was taking part in a just cause. It was not just the right thing to do, but the only thing to do.

By that summer John DeWitt was a soldier undergoing basic training at Camp Dodge, just northwest of Des Moines. He would be one of nearly 115,000 Iowans who would serve during the war, and one of nearly 55,000 who would be shipped overseas. More than 3,500 would die.

He was proud that he volunteered, and in his letters home was disdainful of the men he called "conscripts," the men who served because they were drafted under the new Selective Service Act, signed by Wilson on May 18, 1917.

The American Army he joined in 1917 was small and unprepared for the massive effort in Europe, where millions of European soldiers had been battered by years of fighting. In contrast, the American Army, National Guard, and Marine Corps had a force of only 300,000 men combined.

Congress provided $3 billion, an unheard of sum, to build a new army from office and factory workers, recent high school graduates, and salesmen like John DeWitt and toughen them for what lay ahead in France. More than half of those who served from Iowa were farmers.

So sudden was the call-up, that at first recruits drilled with wooden rifles at some of the new training camps.

My grandfather faced six months of training in the United States before shipping overseas. Physical fitness was essential. He marched for miles, crawled under barbed wire, plunged bayonets into straw dummies, and learned how to put on a gas mask in seven seconds. He learned to use a Springfield rifle, a Browning machine gun, a revolver, and a Browning automatic rifle. Most important. He learned how to follow orders and work with others as a team.

Knowing my grandfather, a devout Catholic, one goal of training was lost on him. Group exercises were intended to keep new inductees busy, tired and away from alcohol and prostitution on rare breaks from camp. His letters home were full of mentions about attending Mass and the comfort he got from doing so. Training officers would not have had to worry about him looking for prostitutes. If he was mocked by fellow soldiers for his chasteness, it would have had no effect on him.

In July, trainees from Camp Dodge, including John DeWitt, traveled to the Iowa State Fairgrounds in Des Moines, where they were sworn into service and received vaccinations and typhoid shots.

They were headed for Europe.

In a letter home from Camp Dodge on August 30, 1917, his twenty-first birthday, my grandfather, his first round of basic training nearly complete, was close to moving on to his next assignment at Camp Mills, on Long Island near New York City. The boy from the small city of Council Bluffs was headed into something entirely alien.

He wrote his mother, as always concerned about his family, especially his father, who was in ill health.

August 30, 1917
Des Moines, Thursday, 3:00 PM

Dearest Mother,

I suppose you and Dad reached home okay, except dead tired. How does Dad feel? I suppose you know that Helen didn't come. Ought to have a letter explaining why this afternoon.

How was everything at home? Did you thank Mrs. Hanson and Helen for the candy? Mrs. Metzger gave me a nice handkerchief. I received that expected package from Helen F. It contained two good sized bath towels and two nice hand towels. They sure are nice. They have JRD sewed on them with red thread—mighty good looking! I am going to write her a nice long letter tonight.

Well Mother dear, this is my long looked for day. I can remember when that seemed years and years away. Tell the girls I got their cards and thank them for me. Does it seem like 21 years ago since I was born, or does it seem longer?

Everything is about the same here. We don't know, yet, when we will go but I think we will start packing Saturday. We put on a big parade yesterday for the Governor. It certainly was some inspiring views and there was certainly some crowd to witness the Pee-rade. They gave us a big hike and drill yesterday morning and again this morning. I just got through washing a pair of pants and patts.

Guess I will have to close this short note as I want to go down and take a shower and besides that, there is nothing new. I am going down to get my picture tonight, so you ought to be getting some of them soon.

Send me two of those suits of BVDs and about three of my soft collars. The highest ones. Send them right away.

We have another addition to our address.
John R. DeWitt
168 Infantry
Company L
84 Brigade
US Expedition Forces
Camp Albert L Mills
Garden City, Long Island, NY

That is after we get away from here. That will cover almost all the envelope. I got a card and letter from Paul today. Will have to close. Hoping to hear from you soon.

As ever, loads of love to all

Camp Dodge, named for Brigadier General Grenville M. Dodge, who organized Iowa's first National Guard unit in 1856, sat eleven miles northwest of Des Moines. Originally built in 1907 as a National Guard training ground, it underwent a massive expansion to accommodate the influx of trainees as America prepared for war.

In late June 1917, shortly before my grandfather arrived, what would become by the war's end a $9.9 million construction effort began. It would create more than twenty miles of dirt roads, more than 150 two-story barracks, a hospital, a power plant, an artillery range, and a one-million-gallon reservoir by the end of the war in November 1918.

John DeWitt was blessed with good luck and impeccable timing. He could have arrived at Camp Dodge in 1916, when troops from there were sent to chase Mexican revolutionary Pancho Villa.

He could have been there in 1918, when the camp was decimated by the Spanish Flu, but he wasn't.

His good sense of timing failed him only when he volunteered, passed the rigorous tests, and won a job as a runner in the trenches, the most dangerous job in a war of dangerous jobs.

The year before my grandfather arrived at Camp Dodge, President Wilson called up the National Guard to keep peace on the Mexican border after revolutionary Pancho Villa raided American territory, in Columbus, New Mexico.

Wilson ordered U.S. Brigadier General John J. Pershing to capture Villa "dead or alive." Pershing, who would go on to lead the American Expeditionary Force in Europe would fail to find Villa.

As part of the effort on the border, Pershing ordered National Guard units that included men from Camp Dodge, to Brownsville, Texas. Eight men would die, all the result of accidents, but the time on the border likely prepared them for the rigors they would face in Europe in 1918.

Men at Camp Dodge would face disaster while my grandfather was fighting in France.

A year later, in October 1918, Camp Dodge would be devasted by the Spanish flu, and Iowans were under quarantine to stop the spread of the lethal virus.

John DeWitt remained in France, in a hospital, the best place to be as the Spanish flu wreaked havoc.

FOUR

A FUTURE PRESIDENT of the United States would echo John DeWitt's sentiments as he prepared for war at Camp Dodge.

On June 22, 1917, shortly after my grandfather volunteered, Harry Truman, twelve years older, accepted a commission as a first lieutenant in an artillery unit of the Missouri National Guard and would go on to fight on the front lines in France.

Truman had volunteered for the war, he said, because "I felt that I was a Galahad going after the Holy Grail."

Those noble ideals aside, as my grandfather continued to write home enthusiastically from Camp Dodge, he was not ready for what awaited in France.

No one was.

The green American troops nicknamed "Doughboys," would have to learn quickly. The dry, neatly cut training trenches, orderly drills, and wooden rifles at Camp Dodge were poor replicas of what was in store in France for John DeWitt. There was no mud, or vermin, or lice or such things as trench foot and trench fever in Iowa.

Fighting in France would push John DeWitt into an alien and hostile new world where the comforts of home he treasured must have seemed unreachable 4,500 miles away as German shells rained down.

In the letters he continued to write home from Camp Dodge, John DeWitt was hungry for the gossip and news of friends, neighbors, and family that anchored him and connected him to his previous life. His letters were full of questions about life in Council Bluffs.

> *How does Dad feel?*
>
> *Received Helen's letter this morning. The circus must have made things lively around there for a couple of days.*
>
> *What did you think of the pictures? Did you send those to Helen Fisher and give Helen I. one and you keep the other big one and one of the bust. I want you to send one of the full to Miss PH Bennett at 813 16th Street, Des Moines, Iowa. Send one to Paul, then I think you will have one left. Isn't that right? I will tell you later who to send that one to.*
>
> *Russell Hughes got married the other day.*
>
> *I got the package yesterday, was glad to get them. I went to Mass yesterday morning. Miss Bennett came out to camp Saturday evening and stayed with Mrs. Head that night and was here until after dinner.*
>
> *The fair is over and things are rather quiet around here now. If you make a big cake and send it down to me, it won't make me mad.*

In France, under fire, watching his comrades die, those comforts would seem very far away.

In May 1917, Woodrow Wilson and Secretary of War Newton D. Baker chose Army General John J. Pershing to lead the American Expeditionary Forces in France.

Pershing faced the enormous challenge of training the surging numbers of ill-prepared new soldiers for combat—some two million by the war's end in 1918. Pershing also had to devise plans to supply the new force and get them across the Atlantic quickly. It was a formidable task, but Pershing would prove up to it. The first American troops would arrive in June, but none would fight until October.

Fatigued English and French troops and their allies have been fighting for more than two years and hoped to use the fresh American troops to fill the increasing number of gaps in their depleted forces.

Pershing would have none of that, decreeing that American soldiers would not serve under foreign control. The Americans would fight on their own.

John J. Pershing had had a long an illustrious military career before that appointment, beginning as the student commander of the West Point honor guard that saluted the funeral train of former president Ulysses S. Grant as it passed the academy in 1885.

As he rose through the ranks, he served in conflicts in the Philippines, where he had been recommended for a Medal of Honor, and in Cuba, where he fought in the Battle of San Juan Hill, made famous by Teddy Roosevelt and his Rough-Riders. Shortly before his appointment to lead the American Expeditionary Forces, Pershing had led the failed American effort to capture Mexican Revolutionary Pancho Villa that included troops from Camp Dodge.

Along the way, Pershing had acquired the nickname "Black Jack," perhaps an excretory appellation that reflected racial attitudes of the time. By some accounts he acquired the name because he had commanded black troops, though others said it was due to his unflinching discipline.

Pershing, like many of his men in France, was sickened to the point of being "reeling and delirious" by the Spanish flu. He would recover in time to attend the signing of the Armistice on November 11, 1918.

Pershing would become a mentor to many leading World War II American generals, including Dwight Eisenhower, Omar Bradley, Douglas MacArthur, and George Patton.

In 1917, though, he faced the suffocating task of getting troops to Europe, ready for combat.

John DeWitt's Iowa National Guard unit, the 168th Infantry, would reach France with Colonel Douglas MacArthur as its chief of staff. The 168th Infantry had become part of a new division, the brainchild of MacArthur, who dubbed the new 42nd the "The Rainbow Division."

With a new army made up of many states' National Guard units, one of Pershing's many dilemmas was avoiding the appearance of favoritism over which troops would have the distinction of being the first to see combat.

MacArthur, in an astute political maneuver, called for combining the Guard units from across the country in one division, the 42nd, which could then be sent to France without slighting any particular state or region.

In proposing the new division, MacArthur described it as a force that would stretch across the United States "like a rainbow." John DeWitt would become part of that rainbow when he joined other troops that would make up the 42nd Division when it assembled at Camp Albert Mills, on Long Island, just outside New York City.

John DeWitt and the rest of the 168th Iowa Infantry departed Camp Dodge for their new training grounds in New York in September. The troop train left Des Moines and headed east as thousands cheered them on. For the quiet, patriotic young man from Council Bluffs, the rousing send-off must have confirmed his decision to volunteer.

As he continued to write his mother every week from Camp Mills, my grandfather had no idea what awaited him, despite training that had provided hints at what was to come. Training in Iowa, hastily devised, did not reflect the reality of modern warfare—rapid-fire artillery, high-explosive ammunition, and battles that left troops hunkered down in deep, often muddy trenches dug to avoid the lethal air above them.

By October 26, John DeWitt would be packed aboard the *US President Grant,* a former passenger liner built in 1907 in Belfast that would by the end of the war make eight round trips across the Atlantic carrying close to 40,000 troops to Europe.

My grandfather's first voyage on the *US President Grant* would be short-lived. Boiler problems would send them back to New York after getting only a third of the way across.

When the Rainbow Division arrived in France that fall, it would face extremes the men had not prepared for, including bitter cold, unheated shelters, and an outbreak of scarlet fever, spinal meningitis and measles before anyone fired a shot.

All that lay ahead for John DeWitt.

It would be from Camp Mills on November 8, shortly before he left for Europe, that he would write home and announce a new assignment that would define his experience in France.

> *Well Mother o' mine, I was promoted to a first class Private yesterday. I know you will be glad because you have mentioned this once or twice. I am also very glad and also because no one can, with any foundation, say I*

> *got it by a pull or by handshaking. Now I don't want this told around at all but this morning the Captain stopped me and told me that I had been picked as a "trench runner". There are four to a company, one for each platoon and I was picked for ours. It will mean a lot of extra work and study. I have to start right in and become proficient in signaling. I have to learn the wig wag system right away. This is a very important position when we get across and in the trenches.*
>
> *That is, we have to carry, send and receive messages from one platoon to another and to and from headquarters.*
>
> *I will have to do a lot of studying and practicing so will have less time than ever to write.*

Despite knowing that the job of trench runner carried with it a very high possibility of death, my grandfather was proud and elated at being chosen. He signed off his note with "Boy Wonder," the only time I saw him brag in his letters.

Camp Mills would open my grandfather's eyes to what else the world had to offer outside Council Bluffs. He'd be exposed to a coarser side of life at Camp Mills, at the time a rapidly growing amalgamation of new troops from cities and small towns across the country, many of whom had different outlooks and different ways of doing things than the church-going and earnest young man from Council Bluffs.

Life at Camp Mills would be an eye-opener for my Grandfather.

True to form, the temptations would not affect him.

John DeWitt went about his preparations, true to his beliefs and strong sense of self and what he wanted to do.

FIVE

WITH CHEERS OF the crowd echoing for the 163rd after his troop train left Des Moines and headed east for Camp Mills, John DeWitt had no idea of life outside Council Bluffs, or the reality of what was in store.

Immediately on the horizon for the young man from Council Bluffs was New York City, exotic and pulsing. With a melting-pot population of more than five and a half million, it was nearly one third larger than that of the entire state of Iowa. Only ten miles from Camp Mills, the metropolis beckoned.

He'd have a taste and in his quiet way, would enjoy New York, despite the abnormally cold weather that would auger one of the worst winters the city had ever experienced.

Next, was a war in France.

New York City offered things he could only imagine.

The war would offer things he would have preferred to have never seen.

In Iowa the war had been a distant rumble. In New York, it was within earshot.

At Camp Mills, he would have ample opportunity to harden his view of the world, to take a more jaundiced approach about the mission he volunteered for and his role in it. He simply could not. It was not his nature.

As he settled into training at Camp Mills, raucous and edgy, sheltered with his company in a large uninsulated tent the makeshift camp provided as quarters, John DeWitt would see a side of life very different from what he was accustomed to. He'd be mixing with other young men from across the United States who formed to become Douglas MacArthur's rainbow. Many were not as genteel. As was his custom, John DeWitt maintained his unflappability. Nothing seemed to deter him or his sense of adventure. He would stand out at Camp Mills, be promoted, and be chosen for the rigorous ordeal of becoming a trench runner.

Camp Mills would be beyond anything the small-city boy had experienced.

The altruistic cause he volunteered for in Council Bluffs was about to take a more threatening turn as the time to depart for France drew closer.

There was much to do and learn, and John DeWitt took it all in stride.

His letters home remained assuring and calm.

To keep up morale, soldiers were encouraged to write home frequently, but it is clear from the volume of letters my grandfather sent from wherever he was, no matter his situation, that John DeWitt did not have to be told to write home. He needed his strong connection to home and Iowa. It is also clear that although all letters from soldiers were censored to prevent sensitive information such as troop movements—time of departure and destinations—John DeWitt was loath to worry his parents, sisters, and friends back home.

He would not have delved into anything that might prompt concern for this safety. His announcement that he'd been chosen as a trench runner, the deadliest assignment a soldier could have, was understated and upbeat.

On October 5, settling into what passed as advanced training, his first note to his mother from Camp Mill was typical. Much, no doubt, was left unsaid, though it was apparent that preparations were underway to get to France.

> *Everything is just fine as always with me.*
>
> *They sure give us plenty of work every day. Went to New York one night last week and saw a lot of the city and had a good time. Hope to go again soon. Our trunks have left and I will enclose the key to the box which ought to get there before long. It will probably be delivered to the house. We have to keep all our things in a bag and it is sure alright, don't know where anything is. We are getting our woolen equipment every day. Got our woolen underwear yesterday. Won't be here over two weeks, I don't think and maybe not that long.*

He was wrong about the date of departure for France. The troops were always the last to know. Still at Camp Mills weeks later, he would have had a better idea of what he was heading into.

Sitting on Long Island ten miles outside the eastern border of New York City, Camp Mills was in September 1917 a slapdash temporary "tent camp" established to train the newly formed Rainbow Division and get it to France as soon as possible. It would eventually grow to accommodate some 40,000 troops. Amenities were scarce, and training was nearly as slapdash as the camp itself.

He took pleasure in simple things.

One was a simple and unexpected gift, a "comfort kit." Assembled by volunteers and paid for by donations from people across the country to groups such as the Red Cross, these kits were sent to recruits in camps across the country. One such group in Minneapolis assembled and distributed 20,000 kits.

The kits signaled in those early days of the American involvement in the war, the enthusiasm and support for the cause that was clearly welcomed by John DeWitt.

On October 5 he wrote:

Dearest Mother,

I received a comfort kit from the Messco girls and it sure is a dandy. It contained a steel mirror, toothbrush, paste, soap, towel, wash rag, comb, batchelor buttons, two spools of thread, white and black, a package of needles, corn cob pipe and tobacco, cigarettes, papers, tablets, six stamped envelopes, pencil, talcum powder, white Vasoline and I don't remember just now what else. Oh yes, a Khaki handkerchief too.

With departure seemingly imminent, my grandfather wrote a long letter home on October 22. Frank and detailed, he discussed his imminent departure for France.

Dearest Mother,

We have not sailed yet and don't know just when we will. Wouldn't be surprised if we went this week or next week and next week will be the latest, I am sure. I feel sure that some of division has left already. There are a lot of mysterious things going on around here. I don't know for sure but I feel sure that they won't allow us to let you know when we sail but will try to let you know somehow so if you get a blank postcard or a card full of nonsense, you will know we have started. Will try and put a

> *number in so you will know the dates. It looks as though we would be moving soon. It is also getting too cold for comfort around these parts. It is cold as the dickens, really have to have an overcoat on to keep warm. They are not giving us any stoves and there is also a bulletin advising us to get our money changed to francs. They have issued passes to New York up until Sunday night so no more passes issued now.*
>
> *My hands are so cold I can hardly write.*

The only certainty was that the cold weather he mentioned frequently was not going away. It was constant.

The men at Camps Mills, in tents with insufficient heat as they readied for France, were on the front edge of an unprecedented winter that would paralyze ports along the Eastern Seaboard, including New York, and at one point storms would extend as far west as Omaha, just across the Missouri River from Council Bluffs.

A series of unrelenting ice storms and blizzards cause food and coal shortages and limit getting critical supplies to the forces in France at a time when they were desperately needed.

The subzero temperatures and blizzards hit when the national rail system was already in crisis, with shortages in coal and rail cars, crucial to getting food and munitions into East Coast ports for shipment to Europe.

The vastly larger problems were condensed into its most basic element for John DeWitt, who wrote his mother on October 22 as the unusually cold weather set in.

> *We have received almost all of the equipment we are going to get. I got three suits of winter underwear issued to me Friday. Not all of us have got them yet but probably*

> *will soon. Haven't put on as yet because they are too hard to wash but if this weather keeps up, I am sure going to put them on. The suits are not very heavy, about as heavy as I wore last winter or just a little lighter.*

He also provided a glimpse of camp life outside of training.

> *Yesterday, Sunday morning, I dislocated the knuckle of my little finger on my left hand playing basketball. It sure is sore and cripples me quite a bit. We didn't get to go to Mass Sunday because we had to stand muster for pay and sign the payroll also.*

Stoved-in finger aside, and despite the cold, his rigorous training, and whatever his thoughts about war, the kind man I was getting to know emerged in that letter. He had much to occupy his thoughts, but he still took the time to seek help for a comrade. In his long letter, John DeWitt would write his mother:

> *There is a fellow in our company who is just the fellow that Miss Spraque would want to adopt. He is from Sioux City. I don't really know much about him except that he gets practically no mail and could use a lot of things as aids to physical comfort. He is very fond of candy and is always buying it and chewing on it. He is a prince of a fellow and everybody likes him. He is real witty and is the life of the tent where he lives. I don't think he has any folks. If he has, they have forgotten they have a son. Tell Ann to be sure to tell Miss Spraque, his name is Harry M. O'Connor, Company L, 168 Division, same address as mine.*

That was the grandfather I remembered as a boy.

SIX

IF THE WAR in Europe seemed abstract and distant to John DeWitt at Camp Dodge, there was much to remind him that it was very real indeed at Camp Mills.

The war was creeping closer.

Training at Camp Dodge, basic in every sense, was only a tease, a brief sip of what was in store for the men of the 163rd. The enormity of the war effort and its acceleration became clearer to him after he arrived on Long Island in early October.

Cracks were beginning to show in the rainbow.

As the time to depart for Europe approached, reality seemed to set in for some soldiers. The playing part—the drills and marching to nowhere with no consequence were ending.

Describing Camp Mills to his mother in early October, he wrote:

> *There are camps all over this island. There must be 150,000 men altogether because there are 40,000 or more in our camp alone. There are two areo-stations real close to our camp. There are machines in the air all day long. We have seen seven in the air at once. They go way up and out of sight and come down in spirals and looping the loop and etc. Sure exciting but we are almost used to them already. We will start drilling Monday unless we*

> *get our exam. We will drill from 7:30 to 11:30 and from 1:05 to 5:00 with ten minutes standing rest each hour. So you can't expect me to write you very often or very much when that starts*

John DeWitt would quickly be confronted with the reality of his future. He was inoculated for diseases alien to his quiet life in Iowa. He would buy a life insurance policy, a jarring purchase for a healthy 21-year old.

For him, though daunting, that was part of the process he had volunteered for.

The war in which they were about to fight was moving from abstraction to reality, and my grandfather noticed the spirits and enthusiasm of some of his comrades were ebbing. There was a growing disenchantment among some soldiers with the war effort he had joined so enthusiastically in the spring.

Unlike many of the things he was confronting, it upset him.

Some of the men were having second thoughts, and scheming for ways to avoid shipping out. While the 163rd was rife with eager volunteers champing at the bit like John DeWitt, others had been drafted under the new Selective Service Act. They had not volunteered and seemed to be starting to resent what was asked of them.

At Camp Mills, my grandfather was appalled, writing home that some fellow soldiers were becoming "yellow."

Courage was sacred to John DeWitt, a foundation on which he thrived throughout the war and took immense pride in.

Men could deliberately fail tests or disobey orders and be tagged as troublemakers and thus unsuitable. Camp Mills had a 500-inmate detention center for such recalcitrants.

The more desperate among them would desert. Between April 1917 and December 1918, shortly after the war ended, American Expeditionary Forces authorities charged 5,558 soldiers for desertion, and convicted 2,657. Twenty-four men were sentenced to death, but had their sentences commuted to prison terms by Woodrow Wilson.

Such things upset my grandfather. In a letter home in early Octobers, he wrote:

> *I don't want you to tell this around but there are sure a lot of the fellows in our company and others who are showing up yellow. They are praying as far as they know how and hoping that they will fail in this next exam we get in the next day or so. It will be the final one before we go across and I am proud to say that I am not one of them. I don't want to go but you will never hear me "holler".*

John Dewitt was ready to do his part, unafraid, no doubt sustained by his Catholic faith and the Holy Communion he took as often as possible.

There would be much to test him in France—many intrusions outside of the bullets and exploding shells that could kill him.

At Camp Mills, he would receive vaccinations against smallpox, cholera, and typhoid—a not-too-subtle message that life in the trenches he would soon inhabit would not be a lark. There was no vaccine against the Spanish Flu, which would decimate troops in Europe and kill some 50 million worldwide. It would devastate the troops at Camp Dodge while my grandfather was in Europe.

At Camp Mills, John DeWitt would have been aware of the squalor of trenches that awaited in France. His letters home make frequent mentions of his correspondence with friends serving elsewhere, and certainly the rumor mill among soldiers at Camp Mills was active if not always accurate.

In his letters home, he mentions his inoculations, though as was his usual practice about not writing anything that would alarm his mother, only briefly.

> *I am able to be up and around. I feel pretty good, all except my arm which is awful painful. This vaccination sure did take. My arm is swollen and have a scab on my arm an inch square.*
>
> *Did I tell you that Ted M. was also sick for a couple of days from his vaccination, but he is up and around today.*

American troop commanders were all too aware of typhoid, which had disastrous consequences for the Army during the Spanish-American War twenty years before. Typhoid shots were mandatory for American soldiers heading to France, and typhoid infections dropped from 142 per 1,000 during the Spanish-American War to one per thousand in World War I.

Though World War I coincided with a global cholera pandemic, a vaccine developed by Louis Pasteur in 1897 was widely available and inoculations were also mandatory.

My grandfather was protected, at least from those diseases. Other conditions he could not control.

He would know by the time he was at Camp Mills what awaited. By then the war was in its third year.

Dirty, cramped, and wet, the dank and miserable trenches, combined with poor nutrition, were the perfect combination for a growing catalogue of conditions that would afflict American soldiers, and vaccinations were not available to prevent them.

Trench foot—numbness, pain, redness and swelling that occurs after standing in cold mud for extended periods was inevitable. Trench foot could lead to gangrene and in extreme cases, amputation. Over the winter of 1914–1915, more than 20,000 British soldiers were treated for trench foot.

Trench fever—severe headache, tenderness or pain in the shin, weakness, anorexia or abdominal pain would infect more than one million troops.

Fear of tuberculosis led to all recruits being screened for the debilitating disease, though later studies would find that at least 10,000 American soldiers served while infected. In 1918, some 150,000 French soldiers were discharged because of tuberculosis.

There was one condition John DeWitt spent no time worrying about.

At Camp Dodge he would have scoffed at the posters and pamphlets extolling the men:

> "Sex Impulse…when controlled or directed, it gives ENERGY, ENDURANCE, FITNESS!"

During the war, the American army would discharge 10,000 men because they had acquired a sexually transmitted disease. A study after the war would find some 415,000 cases of venereal disease out of the three million men who served in the American Expeditionary Forces. Incapacitated and laid up in a camp hospital, men could not fight. The study found that 21,000 soldiers—the equivalent of two infantry brigades—had been unable to fight over an entire year.

Appalled by reports of the first wave of AEF soldiers visiting French brothels, John Pershing ordered them off-limits, noting that he would hold commanders responsible for any venereal disease among their men. Soldiers who failed to report their venereal disease were court-martialed.

For John DeWitt, such warnings and punishments were moot. He was immune to temptation, whether due to his relationship with the mysterious Helen he frequently mentioned or, more likely, his nature.

It is clear he did not have his head in the clouds about his mortality. Life insurance policies, under the Bureau of War Risk Insurance, were available to any soldier and he did not equivocate, despite the cost. Money was constantly on his mind, more so for his struggling family, than himself.

In mid-October, he wrote his mother.

> *Yesterday we were given a chance to sign up for a new war insurance that the government is putting out. At my age, it cost me 65 cents a month for $1,000. The limit we can take is $10,000 that would cost $6.50 a month. When we leave for France we get an increase of 20% in pay, that would be an increase of $6.00 a month in my pay so I took out the limit $10,000 which will cost me $6.50 a month. If I were to get killed, you would not get the $10,000 in a bunch but you would get $57.50 a month for 240 months or 20 years or if I were to be permanently disabled, I would get the $57.50 for the rest of my life besides the pension. That sure is cheap insurance so most of us took the limit.*

A later letter from Camp Mills once again reiterated his concern.

> *I know it must be hard sledding for money and if we ever get any money, I will send you all I can and get along without. I am sure glad the girls have at least started to*

> *school and only hope they can keep a going. The reason I didn't write more often on the trip was because I didn't have anything to write on and you couldn't buy or borrow anything.*

By October 26, my grandfather would be tightly packed aboard the troop ship *US Grant*, thinking he had seen the last of Camp Mills and New York City. Boiler problems would send the *Grant* back after nearly 1,000 miles at sea to anchor in the harbor between the city and Sandy Hook, New Jersey, then to dock for repairs.

John DeWitt would get another chance to train, take in the sights of New York, and explore.

By mid-November he'd be on his way to Europe again, knowing by then he was a trench runner.

The vibrance of the New York City area and all it offered, otherworldly compared to Council Bluffs, was at his fingertips, and John Dewitt planned to make to the most if it.

SEVEN

THE COUNTRY WAS awash in a wave of patriotic fervor, and autumn 1917 was a good time to be a soldier walking about New York City in a uniform bearing the distinctive patch of the Rainbow Division.

In August, a month before my grandfather arrived at Camp Mills, hundreds of thousands of New Yorkers lined five miles of Fifth Avenue from 110th Street to the Washington Square Arch in lower Manhattan to cheer New York's marching 27th Infantry, part of the Rainbow Division.

By then, Camp Mills had become a tourist attraction.

As summer turned to fall, the ramshackle training ground offered at least one thing its chilled residents enjoyed—adulation and attention that made their long nights in drafty tents seem almost worthwhile. Soldiers worn from their dayslong drilling were routinely greeted by cheering citizens from New York City and surrounding towns and states who thronged to the camp for weekend parades.

By late September, when my grandfather arrived, 60,000 civilians had visited. It was not only people from New York City. A survey by a *New York Times* reporter of the camp's parking lots turned up plates from Pennsylvania, Virginia, Maryland, and Illinois.

Thousands of spectators cheered on September 22 as Secretary of War Newton D. Baker reviewed a parade of the entire 26,000-member Rainbow Division—more than twice as large as the entire American Army during the Spanish American War.

It took forever. My grandfather marched and wrote home about it.

> *I am enclosing a clipping telling of the big review we took part in last Sunday. It surely was some sight. It was over four hours for the parade to pass the Secretary. Miles and miles of soldiers.*

On October 8, another parade at Camp Mills was cheered on by 75,000 people. According to *The New York Times*, 5,000 cars parked outside the parade grounds. The phenomenon attracted so much attention the State of New York liquor commission began a crackdown on unlicensed sales.

Soldiers out on the town attracted the glowing admiration of locals, and for my modest grandfather, induced a certain aura of pride. In uniform, he was a hero. For a young man who never sought attention, his new celebrity must have put a wry smile on his face as he walked the streets of New York.

I know this about my grandfather, not only from his letters but the older man I spent time with as a boy. He was not starstruck by what he encountered. If his perilous time under fire in France didn't affect him, the Big City and the training for the impending war would not either. He was no hayseed craning his neck at the 60-story Woolworth Building on Broadway, then the world's tallest, or the iconic 22-story Flatiron Building in Times Square.

Reading his letters home, I was stuck by his nonchalance over his fate and his impending mission. He had a steely ability, it seemed, to block out the future and live in the moment. If I did not know better, his stories sounded more like a kid writing home from summer camp than a man about to go to war.

I began to understand the older Grampa I knew and why he never crowed about his time in France when he returned to Iowa and picked up his life after the war.

He had a job to do in France and he did it, proud that he never shied away from it, that he was not among those who had turned "yellow" under pressure.

For John Dewitt, there was nothing more to it. Stoicism was his strong suit.

He simply carried on, impressed by sights unimaginable in Council Bluffs. In New York, he was immersed in a simmering, melting pot of cultures and religions and languages from around the world. The landlocked Iowan was surrounded by water—Long Island Sound, the East and Hudson Rivers, the vast Atlantic, countless bays and estuaries—and architecture the likes of which he'd never seen. When he returned to Council Bluffs after the war, he was amused, I'm sure, by the construction of the city's tallest building, the seven-story, brick Bennett Building, erected in 1923.

When he got the opportunity to step away from Camp Mill and escape the rigors of training, he did, and he would find joy in doing so.

From his letters, it is clear to see he was intrigued but not overwhelmed. He merely drank it in as part of a new experience.

Free time was precious and rare at Camp Mills, and announcements about a chance to stand down were last-minute. That was clear from one note home shortly after he arrived.

> *Tomorrow is Sunday. Haven't heard as yet whether we will be able to go to Mass or not but I hope so.*

On October 5, he wrote for the first time of the city, but was spare on details.

> *They sure give us plenty of work every day. Went to New York one night last week and saw a lot of the city and had a good time. Hope to go again soon.*

Devout as he was, my grandfather liked having a good time, and when he had the opportunity, he made the most of it. I learned later that my grandfather enjoyed a drink or two as an older man. I never noticed as a kid, so it was not a major part of his personality. I have no doubt that on leave he was not a stranger to having a few if the occasion merited it. He never mentioned those occasions to his mother. Dutiful son that he was, he didn't want to worry his mother. Some things are best left unsaid.

My grandfather had no shortage of friends to accompany him on his jaunts outside Camp Mills. His Iowa sensibility and easygoing nature assured he was not alone on his adventures in and around the Big City. The optimism and unflappability that came through in his letters, his rare complaints, drew others to him. He was like the eye of a hurricane, a calm haven for friends while everything roiled around them.

On one excursion he saw for the first time the Atlantic Ocean he would soon be crossing, twice. He and a group of friends visit Playland at Rockway Beach in Queens, an attraction the usually drew thousands on hot summer days. In the chilly fall air, the scene was slower paced, but exciting. As a proud Irish American, he might have been amused that Rockaway would later be facetiously dubbed the "Irish

Riviera" because of the large concentration of Irish-Americans from the city drawn to its beaches.

> *Saturday night a bunch of us got a machine and went out riding. We went to Rockaway Beach. That is a big amusement place next to Coney Island. Sure would like to see it when it was going full blast. It is practically closed now though. Rockaway is some swell place. There are certainly some places all around here. Rockaway is about 20 miles from here. I had my first view of the ocean. It certainly was one wonderful, never to be forgotten, sight! There was a beautiful moonlight night, full moon and almost as light as day. We ran along the beach on the sands packed almost as hard as the pavement. The waves came rolling up. I got my feet wet and washed my hands. I also got a big shell I picked up.*

He would board the *US Grant* on October 18 with 5,000 other Rainbow Division soldiers in what would be an aborted trip to France, thinking it was the last he'd see of New York City and the country he was defending, at least for a while.

He wrote to his mother of the passage out of New York Harbor.

> *We had a most wonderful view of New York, wonderful skyline and everything that you hear and read of New York.*
>
> *After we started to sea, we had another view of the Statue of Liberty all lit up. It was sure some sight*

On October 29, after his ill-fated voyage on the *Grant* would once again deposit him at Camp Mills, he wrote admiringly of the city again, that now bore the traces of military action.

After the ship, President Grant, stayed anchored in the channel for two hours, we moved up to the number six pier at Hoboken (we loaded onboard at number three pier on our way out) and unloaded and marched onboard a ferry and went to Long Island City, loaded on the train and out to Camp Mills again, of course all this took time.

When we unloaded off the ship, we marched past several other big transports and were scared to death that they were going to load us right onboard another vessel and ship us right back.

We were sure a happy bunch when we marched onto the ferry. It was sure a wonderful trip from Hoboken to Long Island City seeing New York skyline at night. We didn't leave the pier at Hoboken until 7:00 PM. We could see all the buildings lit up at night, the Woolworth, the Singer, the Metropolitan Life, the Flatiron,and etc and we also could see all the different ferries, tug boats, pleasure vessels, ocean going liners, sub chasers, revenue cutters, fire boats and police patrol boats.

Just wonderful sights, all the big bridges, Brooklyn, Manhattan, Queensboro, 59th street and etc., Colgate's big sign and the clock and just any number of similar things. It sure was glorious to see land and humans again, especially women.

He closed with a reminder that, while he might have missed his Helen, he did appreciate the social advantage of being a man in uniform. He was still a young man, after all.

Didn't see a woman for 10 days, and most of all to get our feet on Mother Earth once more. That sure is a grand and glorious feeling.

My grandfather was not above a bit of clandestine raiding to make the most of his experience outside of training. Back at Camp Mills, still waiting for orders for Europe, and still freezing, he told his mother of one such effort.

A big bunch of troops left this camp on their way across and we raided their camp and got a table and a stove, and believe me, we need it. We pretty near froze last night. I slept with my overcoat on and I was alright but my feet. We didn't have any straw in our tents and that helps a lot. A few of us got straw today and I am one of the few so I expect to sleep warm tonight. Our tent is nice and warm with the stove going. We may get to have electric lights in our tents. We have them all wired but haven't any juice as yet but hope to get it soon. If we get them, we will have a regular home.

He enjoyed the hijinks, and boys being boys, he was still awake at 1:30 one morning writing his mother of another foray.

Oh I forgot to tell you in the other letter, and I almost forgot in this one, about my having the keenest bed in the company.

When Alabama left, of course, we all went over to their camp and raided it for household necessities, everybody getting all they could use and carry. I found a set of springs that some officer had owned. I also got a table, a big wash pan, a couple of brooms, a couple links of stovepipe, three or four wash pans and a big pan from the kitchen. So I loaded them all on the springs and bent the hook on the coat hanger for a handle and away we go! I dragged the whole outfit from their camp up our regiment street and down to my tent. They sure did laugh as I went by.

I put the springs on my cot and it is just the right size. Then I put my tich of straw over that, then my blankets and I have a real bed. I am the only one in the company and there are only two or three in the regiment. The boys all envy me. The only trouble is that it is so nice that when I lay down, I have an awful time getting up. I'll sure hate to leave it when we go.

Other adventures must have triggered a moral dilemma for my pious grandfather.

Dearest Mother O' mine,

I didn't get to finish this letter Friday night because Weary and the gang came in and wanted me to go on a chicken stealing expedition. They wouldn't let me write. They took my candle away and then they hid my letter. After I found it, they wouldn't let me write so I had to go with them. We came back with two chickens. They were skinned and cleaned and cooked, roasted over the fire. Then they got through about 12:30. I didn't eat any but I went to bed after we got back but they wouldn't let me sleep until they went to bed.

I wondered if he didn't eat—unusual for him—because he was tired or because of the guilt of stealing a poor farmer's chickens.

His lighthearted letters showed his singular ability to shut out distractions and focus on the now, a key strength of his survival later in France, I've decided.

Another focus was food.

The nervous stomachs common to many soldiers facing combat was alien to him. My grandfather loved to eat, a lifetime affection. Concern about the war did not affect his appetite.

Returning to Camp, surely exhausted and emotionally spent after the *Grant* turned around, he wrote glowingly about his favorite pastime.

> *We marched into camp through mud and water up to our shoe tops and through water up to our knees several times. The wind was blowing to beat the band, a lot of the tents were half down and water in most of them. The company street was almost a lake but I didn't hear anyone crabbing. They were all so glad to get back.*
>
> *Poston, Curley, Cam and I took our packs off, threw them down in the mud and water and lit out for a friend's house in Hempstead. We knew them before we left. We got there about 12 PM. They were just going to retire when our wet crew hit. They were sure pleasantly surprised to see us and they started a fire in the kitchen stove and we took off our wet clothes and put on some dry ones that Poston had left with them before he left.*
>
> *After we got warm and had related our experiences, we went and put on our clothes which had dried and didn't get up until about 8:00. We had a breakfast like I had often dreamed about since I left home. Porkchops, pancakes, batter and syrup and coffee. Gee but that was a*

treat. We sat and ate until we could eat no more! Then we came out to camp, straightened around our things, cleaned our guns and bayonets which were in awful condition and required about two hours work on them.

After retreat, we went back to these people's house and had a real dinner, the first since I left home and, oh, but it did taste good (roast beef, mashed potatoes, gravy, peas, spaghetti, turnips, head lettuce, pickled pears, bread and butter and coffee).

Eating was a common theme. In later letters, still waiting for orders to France, he wrote often and enthusiastically about food:

Just got through eating dinner and it wasn't bad, had potatoes, roast beef, gravy, hardtack , tomatoes, bread and coffee.

Oh joy, oh boy!! Those cookies and candy—gee but they were good. I ate almost all of both of them alone, only giving a few of them away! Those cookies were the best I ever tasted and the candy. Say if Ann made that candy, she is sure a world beater. I have a few crumbs of the candy left.

Weary and I just got back from town. We went to confession and are going to

Communion in the morning if nothing happens. This is the first time we have gone to this church. It certainly is a fine church, although not very big. They say they feed the soldiers after Mass in the morning. Here's hoping!

I received a letter yesterday and the day before from Helen F. and today I received a box of about three dozen donuts.

They certainly are good although they are just a little dry. They don't know what donuts are in this part of the country. They have what are called crullers, which are somewhat similar.

After Mass all soldiers were invited to a KC Hall where they were served breakfast by girls and women of the church. It was certainly a nice breakfast, ham and eggs, creamed potatoes, bread and butter, cake, jam, jelly and coffee. It was certainly a nice meal and Mother, we ran out of jam at our table and I asked one of the women if we could have some more and she said "you bet you can Sunny Boy". Gee but I was surprised and after we got through eating, I got to talking to her and told her I bet she had a boy in the Army. She answered yes, she has a boy 19 in France now.

Food and his great joy in describing it—reliving the experiences of his various meals and treats belied the fact that the time to leave was approaching. It must have been on his mind, though he never wrote of his concerns, if he had any. Those he kept to himself.

One letter home shortly before he boarded the transport that would take him to the war, revealed one thing that must have been on his mind, the mysterious Helen.

Haven't heard from Helen I. since I wired her. Please call if they have a phone and see if you can get a hold of Grace and see what you can find out.

By mid-November he was back at sea, heading for France, this time on a more commodious ship this second trip.

His last letter home before he landed, was headed "Somewhere on the Atlantic, on a pleasant Sunday night."

The war was closing in, the time for hijinks was over. There would be no reprieve this time.

> *We reached the danger zone this morning but have seen nothing of the expected convoy as yet. Starting today we have to wear our life preservers all the time we are away from our own bunks. Until today we could carry them. Starting tonight we have to sleep with our clothes on. In other words, we have to be fully dressed at all times.*

EIGHT

IF JOHN DEWITT'S time under fire in the trenches offered his most likely opportunity to die, his two Atlantic crossings came in a close second.

He sailed 4,300 miles on two trips aboard lumbering troopships to reach France. Each mile after leaving the safety of New York Harbor increased the chance of being torpedoed by a German U-boat.

More than two million American soldiers and 7.5 million tons of cargo were carried to France during the nineteen months the United States was involved in World War I. Seventy-five percent of the ships heading for France would depart from New York, the city's skyline and the Statue of Liberty the last of America the soldiers aboard would see before their lives would change radically.

John Dewitt's first voyage began on October 18, when he boarded the *USS President Grant* along with 5,000 troops, 500 officers, and a complement of 500 sailors, escorted by a seven-ship convoy.

The war became real aboard the *Grant*.

In a letter home from the deck of the *Grant* after a week at sea, my grandfather wrote his mother of what was a daily practice:

The convoy of seven ships had a guard of two torpedo boat destroyers and the Battleship Seattle.

Monday afternoon our ship had target practice. Our ship is equipped with four 5 inch guns, two forward and two aft, and also two 1 pound guns mounted on the second deck, up just a little forward of the middle of the ship.

When it starts to get dark, all lights are out and no smoking on deck. I will enclose a slip that was handed to us as we came onboard called "instructions for troops".

Our ship swung out and let the rest of the fleet pass. Then we swung in behind them and the ship in the rear and to the south of us dropped out the target on a rope.

The forward guns fired first and fired about five times before they made a sure hit. The target was real small, just about the size of a periscope.

They came real close but didn't hit it until the fifth shot. Then the rear gun fired and the gunner on that is one of the best gunners in the Navy and he hit it the first shot and blew it all to pieces. Then he fired at the base twice more and sure hit it. They certainly do make a noise.

The convoy that accompanied the *Grant* included two torpedo boat destroyers and a battleship, part of an American strategy to reach Europe safely. By 1917, the Germans had refined their successful submarine campaign to stop men and supplies from reaching the French battlefields, where its armies were failing.

As my grandfather sat on the *Grant*'s deck writing home, German U-boats were waiting.

On February 1, 1917, Kaiser Wilhelm II, by then in power for twenty-nine years, approved an order to unleash "unrestricted" submarine warfare on merchant shipping to aid Germany's flagging efforts in the war. The month before, Britain had lost forty-nine ships. After the Kaiser's edict, German submarines would sink 105 British ships in February and 147 in March. The new aggression would include ten American merchant ships, a devastating loss that would play a major role in changing President Woodrow Wilson's staunch advocacy for neutrality. Wilson campaigned on keeping America out of the war.

By April, The United States would enter the war.

By late spring, as my grandfather was deciding to enlist, U-boats would begin attacking American ships bringing troops from the American Expeditionary Force to Europe.

From April 1917 until the war's end, U-boats would sink 200 American vessels. Fast and maneuverable, at least relative to many of the retrofitted ships called into action as transports, U-boats could cruise under water at a depth of 165 feet, had a cruising range of 25,000 miles, and carried 16 self-propelled torpedoes. U-boat commanders often attacked merchant ships on the surface, seizing supplies, then scuttling the ship, sending it to the bottom. Germany sank some 5,000 merchant ships during World War I, killing approximately 15,000 Allied sailors to die and not even make it there to participate.

The *President Grant* was not designed to transport massive amounts of soldiers. A diagram my grandfather included in his letter showed how tightly soldiers were packed into hastily constructed bunkbeds along the inside of the *Grant*'s hull. There was row upon row of beds, one on top of the other, with little more than two feet of clearance to the bunk above, the gurgle of the passing Atlantic only inches away.

The *Grant* had been a luxury ocean liner. Built in Belfast in 1907 for the Hamburg-America Line, it had spent seven years in commercial service before it found itself confined in New York in August 1914, when Word War I erupted. When America joined the war in April 1917, it was seized by the U.S. government and turned over to the Navy. Interesting that they had the power to do that.

The Navy had to act quickly after America entered the war. Its first effort to avoid the threat of German submarines was assembling a fleet of four cruisers, thirteen destroyers, two yachts fitted with guns, and two fuel tankers. The new fleet would in early June 1917 escort fourteen ships carrying soldiers and supplies to France.

The *Grant* would later become part of that improvised navy.

The *Grant*'s comfortable days as a luxury ocean liner were over, and John DeWitt made note of his accommodations.

> *We are sure crowded on this boat. It was a fright the first few days. The men are getting used to it by now but they sure did cuss and crab and kick. In a way they have us in here like cattle and until they got a little system, they herded us the same way.*
>
> *It certainly is awful to try to sleep down here. The air is very foul and has been too hot for comfort, which I couldn't stand so every night I have sneaked out on the deck and gone to sleep. They run us all below at 9:00 PM. I have a secluded corner where I have been sleeping without being disturbed except once when I sneaked right back.*

In another note home, part whimsical, part darkly informative, he recalled portions of the voyage.

When we were at sea we saw flying fishes, porpoises and one whale. You may be sure that when we saw the porpoises, I thought of that old song that Dad used to sing to me when I was a mere lad.

I also forgot to tell you the joke of us having to wear our life preservers or life absorbers—we call them. They were like two small pillows tied together on one side with enough room between them to stick our head through and with strings on the bottom of them to be around our middle. We had to wear them all the time we were away from the bunks. We even had to wear them at our meals or we didn't eat. Can you imagine standing up eating with two sofa pillows tied together and one in front and one in the back? It was a grand and glorious feeling—not!!

Those "life absorbers" were more likely designed for psychological comfort than for practicality. Immersed in the cold November waters of the North Atlantic, a soldier would have at most ninety minutes before dying of hypothermia, often less.

As always, my grandfather made note of the food, and he left little doubt meals were somewhat more pedestrian than the seven-course repasts served by tuxedo-wearing waiters during the ship's headier days.

I was fortunate in getting a permanent detail onboard guarding at one of the mess halls during meal time. They only feed us twice a day, although the sailors and officers eat three times a day. The food is fair, that is all that can be said of it. Being special on guard, we get to eat first and can eat all we want and we sure do eat until the rest of the boys and make them jealous. Oftentimes they don't get enough to satisfy them.

Over the course of the war, the *Grant* would make eight-round transatlantic voyages, transporting some 40,000 men to the war, but John DeWitt's voyage was not one of them. Boiler problems would send them back to New York.

Monday night, about 7:30 PM, our ship turned around and started back for New York. At the time we turned around, we were about 1,000 miles out. It is only 3,300 miles across.

If my grandfather was disappointed, his feelings soon rebounded at the sight of New York again.

Last night, Friday, we passed Sandy Hook. At present, Saturday morning at 11:00, we are anchored somewhere between Sandy Hook and New York.

We can see land on both sides of us and buildings and everything and, believe me, it sure is a welcome sight to see land once more. It is a peach of a day. The sun is shining bright and it is cold, really an ideal day. We are in a channel and boat and tugs are passing going both ways. We have seen French and British vessels going by, their sides and smokestacks and everything painted different colors and painted to represent waves. It is called camouflage, I believe. Part of everyday language now We don't know what they are going to do or anything else.

Back in New York, morale was mixed and feelings uncertain. Rumors were rampant. Despite the disruption, the mysterious Helen reappeared in his thoughts.

> *There have been a million different rumors of what they are going to do with us. One of them is that we were going to go back to Des Moines and act as military police over the conscripts.*
>
> *It is now rumored that we will disembark this afternoon but we know nothing for sure. I will try and get the letters mailed. I may not get a chance. After you get through reading this, mail it at once to Helen in Davenport, Ohio.*
>
> *The bunch were sure a happy bunch yesterday and are worse today.*

Back at Camp Mills, on November 8, 1917, the day "The Boy Wonder" wrote his mother from Camp Mills to announce he'd been chosen as a trench runner, the front page of *The New York Herald* was bursting with news about the war he was about to join.

Attacks by the menacing *Unterseeboots* by then were common, so much so that another *Herald* headline story that day stated,

ONLY EIGHT BIG SHIPS ARE SUNK BY THE U BOATS

The *Herald* also carried news of what awaited him. The Italians were retreating from a German assault near the Tagliamento River and calling for American and Allied assistance. In France, seven aviators were lost in thick fog. In Budapest, rioters pillaged city shops, and in the Middle East, the British had taken Gaza on its way to Jerusalem.

Most ominous for John DeWitt as he prepared to board his second troopship to Europe, was news that the 265-foot U.S. Navy patrol boat *Alcedo* had been torpedoed by a German U-boat off the coast of France and sunk, killing twenty-one crewmembers.

Back at Camp Mills after the *Grant's* return, John DeWitt would once again immerse himself in the rigorous training for his new trench-runner assignment. After the failed passage on the *Grant* and with rumors flying, news of the U-boats certainly would have reached John DeWitt. Given what I knew about my grandfather, the unsettling headlines would have meant nothing.

He was on a mission.

The *Herald's* account of the sinking of the *Alcedo* would have provided a dark hint for John DeWitt about the fragility of that mission. He knew by then that the war in France would be brutal and unforgiving. He did not know that getting there would offer its own dire challenges.

DREXEL YACHT ALCEDO IS SUNK, 21 LOST

The *Alcedo,* a luxury craft formerly owned by Philadelphia philanthropist and newspaper publisher George W. C. Drexel had been pressed into service by the U.S. Navy, which had been unprepared and caught short-handed for the massive effort brought on after America entered into the war.

Purchased by the U.S. Navy June 1, 1917, the *Alcedo* had been conducting anti-submarine and escort patrols near the French coast on November 4 when it was torpedoed and sunk. One officer and twenty sailors were killed in the explosion or drowned as the *Alcedo* sank quickly. The rest of the crew and its commanding officer took to two boats, rowing. One boat was picked up by a French patrol. The second was towed to safety by French fishermen.

Eleven days later, the U.S. Navy destroyers *Fanning* and *Nicholson* would become the first American ships to respond to the growing U-boat campaign when they captured and scuttled a German submarine off the southwest coast of

Ireland on November 17, a day when my grandfather would be back at sea again on his second attempt to reach France.

The perils of the Atlantic crossing were likely the last thing on his mind when John DeWitt arrived at Camp Mills in September, where the basic training he'd undergone in Iowa would accelerate, and where he would excel.

Being chosen as a trench runner, regarded as an essential and thankless assignment that meant almost certain chance of death, spoke highly of John DeWitt's tenaciousness.

Running crucial messages through and across the labyrinth of trenches dug into the war zone required fitness, stamina, a quick and adaptive mind and an acute sense of direction in a landscape that changed by the hour as shells rained down. Trench runners had to be tough and quick-witted enough to find their destinations in any type of weather. They had to be able to swiftly get through or over any obstacle along the way after they left the safety of their command posts.

If they were fortunate enough to deliver their messages, they had to be able to get back, all the while avoiding sniper fire and incoming shells.

As a newly promoted private first class, John DeWitt would be putting his life on the line for $30 a month, the equivalent of $550 today. He never complained about the inequity and continued to send half his check to his parents.

By November 12, it was clear they'd be heading out again soon. There would be no return to Camp Dodge as some rumors had indicated. In my grandfather's mind, I'm sure he felt those rumors were the product of the men he felt were "yellow." He would have ignored them.

He was ready to go and feeling good about it.

I was issued a new hat yesterday, a pair of leggings and some new shoestrings so I feel pretty much dressed up. Oh boy! I am starting to feel at home in a uniform now. It is about time.

Well Mother dear, I will have to close but will try and drop you another short note before we go onboard.

Loads and loads, oceans and oceans of love to all. Flocks and flocks of hugs and kisses also to you one and all.

As always,
Sunny Boy

The date on his next letter was blacked out. He was on a new ship "Somewhere on the Atlantic." Letters were being censored, and my grandfather could not write when they left New York nor name "the northern port" where they stopped. He was once again in U-boat territory, and while the unnamed transport carrying him offered much better living conditions than that of the *Grant*, the war was closing in. Restrictions on what he could write were harsh.

We left on the [censored] *and are still on the ocean, although we went to a northern port and laid there a couple or three days. We reached the danger zone this morning but have seen nothing of the expected convoy as yet. Starting today we have to wear our life preservers all the time we are away from our own bunks. Until today we could carry them. Starting tonight we have to sleep with our clothes on. In other words, we have to be fully dressed at all times.*

There are [censored] *and they have* [censored] *for a fare you well. We are supposed to reach* [censored] *on* [censored]. *I think, or at least it is rumored, that we will get a period of training in* [censored].

This has been a splendid trip compared to the other. We have lots more room, better food and, in fact, everything is better. Very few of the boys have been sick. As for myself, I have felt fine every minute of the trip except one day when I was bothered with a very sore throat but this is almost well now.

By then, after all he had been through in the tumultuous months since he enlisted, he was in the thick of it, and sent a gentle reminder to his mother that life in Council Bluffs was far from the tensions in Europe. Writing about the young deck crew, he made a subtle appeal that I think he wanted his mother to share with friends and neighbors.

You should see the mere lads on board who are doing men's work. They are not any bigger than our 10–12 year olds but they are 15 and 16, at least that is what they say. They carry cans almost as big as they are. That is what brings home the fact that there is a war. The people of the U.S. do not realize that we are at war but I think the realization will be brought home to them very soon.

He was still concerned about Helen and her fading attentions, apparently.

Write Helen and let her know that you heard from me or send her this letter if you will.

True to form, he was still up for his usual hijinks and still writing about food.

> *Have certainly had a lot of fun this trip. A bunch of us fellows have a gang and we sure do put on some stunts. We will eat our Thanksgiving dinner onboard. We had a chicken for dinner today and have hopes of a big dinner Thanksgiving.*
>
> *A couple of us fellows are slickers I and we have eats that other fellows dream about. Lots of love to all and best wishes to all. Be sure and write often.*

By December 3 he was in Winchester, England, some 14 miles inland from Southampton, where his ship mostly likely put in after the Atlantic voyage.

He made only brief mention of the U-boat perils and the war, then returned to safer topics.

> *We managed to escape the subs alright, having us a couple of fairly close calls.*
>
> *We have found out a lot of interesting news about "over there" from fellows that have been through the mill and returned. Some of them have been injured and some on special detail.*
>
> *We are in the air raid district. There have been raids near us but not lately*

He was in an entirely new world from the Council Bluffs he'd left eight months before as a young traveling salesman. Despite his destination in France, he was having the time of his life.

We landed safely at one of England's largest ports after being on the boat for seventeen days. It was certainly some trip. This being my third day to have seen quite a bit of the country. We traveled from our port of landing to our present camp by train in the nighttime, thereby missing out on seeing about 200 miles of England. What we did see was sure interesting. We do not expect to be here much more than a week before we go across. It is very little that we are permitted to tell.

In Europe after dodging the U boat perils, about to see combat, it would not be a letter home if he did not continue to write about food—and Helen.

The food on the boat was just fair and that is all, although we did get turkey on Thanksgiving Day. It was fair and that is all. We certainly did miss out on our usual big feed on that day. We all thought about what we would have been doing and eating if we were at home.

Wish you make some oatmeal cookies or something that will stand up and still be good to eat, even if they are hard.

The food we are getting is sure poor and the quantity is minus. We generally get up hungry but will get better when we get to France.

We are allowed five slices of war bread a day but it is sure good.

Send this letter to Helen, will you please? I will try and find time to write you both from now on.

NINE

THE GLIDDEN *Graphic*'s November 8 headline spread atop a front page devoted entirely to the horrible news.

GLIDDEN BOY FIRST AMERICAN KILLED IN FRANCE

At Camp Mills after the aborted voyage of the *President Grant*, my grandfather had certainly heard. His mother and father in Council Bluffs would have known by then as well.

The entire country was waking to the news. I grew up in Iowa hearing the name "Merle Hay" all the time. The pop radio station we listened to KIOA based in Des Moines had ads all the time for stores in "The Merle Hay Plaza." The name meant nothing to me.

Merle Hay, a 21-year-old from Glidden, Iowa, was among the first three Americans to die in the war in Europe. Hay was killed near the French village of Artois two days before. He had volunteered in May, trained at Fort Bliss, Texas, after a brief stop in Colorado and had arrived in France with the first American Expeditionary Force troops as part of the 16th Infantry Regiment in June. Black Jack Pershing's hurried plan for inserting troops into battle had called for further training in Europe, and whatever Hay learned once he arrived would have to suffice.

The graphic details of Hays's death would not be revealed in the national coverage of the ominous milestone until years later. Gruesome facts were not part of any newspaper story at the time, especially about the war in Europe. The war effort, and the need for citizen support was paramount. But any soldier heading to France would know. The rumor mill was far too efficient to let the details pass.

Hay had been posted in the trenches some 500 yards from the enemy position when the German assault began in the pre-dawn hours of November 3. The Germans blasted holes with explosives in the barbed wire that served as a fragile barrier, shelled the Americans, then overran them.

Merle Hay, James Gresham, and Thomas Enright, part of an outnumbered company cut off from reinforcements, engaged in hand-to-hand combat with the Germans. A survivor recalled seeing Hay fighting two Germans with his bayonet. American help arrived fifteen minutes later to find Hay, Gresham, and Enright dead, and five others wounded. A dozen other Americans were captured.

Hay had been shot in the head with a 9-millimenter pistol and his throat had been slit.

Hay and my grandfather, the same age, had enlisted in Iowa at the same time and it seemed that geographic determination played a part in the fates. Glidden was 108 miles northeast of Council Bluffs but each young man went in different directions. What little training Hay had undergone was in Colorado and Texas. He had arrived in France while my grandfather was still in his early days at Camp Dodge.

On one hand, Hay's death was a stark indication of the confusion and lack of a coherent training program for the American effort.

On the other, it was a reminder that John DeWitt's charmed life had once again prevailed.

The response to Hay's death captured the mood of the country, and that of my grandfather. Service was a higher cause, the American effort an altruistic quest.

In April, shortly before Merle Hay enlisted, the *Graphic* had run an editorial stating that, "Up to the present time, to the best of our knowledge, no young man from Glidden has enlisted. Every town and community will be expected to furnish its share of young men for army and navy service that our enemy across the seas may be brought to terms as speedily as possible."

"If it has been necessary that he lay down his life for his country, I'm proud of the boy," Merle Hay's own bereft father told reporters after learning his son had been killed.

Hay's company commander would write of his death:

"He was a faithful soldier, one we could trust. At all times his work was of high quality but especially at the time of his death did he prove his true worth. He stayed at his post of duty and fought to the last. We are proud of the true American spirit shown by him and his comrades."

I began to understand the tone of my grandfather's letters home, why he maintained his upbeat reports despite the darker side of what he had found himself immersed in. He was protecting the innocence of his proud family. He had chosen very early in his military career to not cause unnecessary anxiety for his safety. His family was too precious, and too proud of his service to describe the hell he was beginning to taste.

He kept things on a higher plane.

Years later, back in Iowa and practicing law, he would write to my mother Maribeth while she was away at college, recounting how the 163rd camped next to a group of French troops making the best of the wine sold at the camp exchange.

Everyone had gotten drunk, he wrote. He didn't mention to my mother whether he was among them, but I imagine he was.

He did not mention the incident in his letters home to his mother after he arrived in France.

He did not mention the rain and cold and the mud of the trenches, nor the trench foot and the disease brought on by what had to have been a miserable existence.

He did not mention Merle Hay.

He was doing well, he'd write repeatedly.

Some things were better left unsaid.

TEN

SLOWLY STUDYING MY grandfather's letters, frustrated at his reticence to write home and open up about what he was actually going through, I had an epiphany of sorts, sparked by a single comment to his mother in a letter dated December 18 and mailed from France.

The answer had been in front of me the entire time, but it took until I carefully reread that letter that I understood what he was planning to do.

It was obvious to me by then that he wanted to protect his mother from the unspoken agreement they shared. He would never describe to her or his sisters what he was going through. That was why he never mentioned Merle Hay, nor the men from Council Bluffs who were killed in a gas attack in May 1918. It was why he never went into detail of the deadly realities of his job as a trench runner, or the fetidness of his new surroundings.

All was well, he'd write. He was having the time of his life.

While he was honing his edge for the war, getting his mind right, he was still the amiable John DeWitt, writing home about enjoying the sights or entertaining his family with a reference to his sister and her school teacher back in Council Bluffs.

> *Tell Ann to be sure to tell Miss Reed that I have seen King Arthur's Roundtable and etc. Also the grave of Isaac Walton, where Queen Mary was married and etc. Also Winchester College. This town is the oldest town of any consequence in England. It is certainly the home of historical happenings and etc.*

He'd write of Ireland, his parents' homeland, a connection that would be sure to elate them.

As always, he'd write about food, or the lack of it, and he'd ask for small comforts, like tobacco and shaving gear.

> *If you didn't send 10 sacks of Bull Durham and about three tea towels, then send at once. Then try and send me 5 sacks every two weeks.*

But he rarely mentioned the war. He would hint at it, make vague references, but he would never go into specifics to his mother, frequently telling her not to worry. Still in England on December 6 waiting for transport to France, he had written home:

> *Wounded soldiers or crippled soldiers can be seen almost everywhere you turn.*

Adding,

> *I have certainly seen a lot of interesting sights and talked to a number of soldiers who have been through the mill.*

By the time he wrote on December 18, which he headed "SOMEWHERE IN FRANCE," he was no longer an idle tourist. He was a young soldier at war.

> *Do not worry about me because I know of old that I will make it out alright so don't worry for one little minute as I still wear that smile. I am feeling fine and in good health. Tell Dad that I will be able to swap yarn for yarn when I get back.*

That's when it hit me. When he returned—and it was never *if* he returned—he'd share the darker details with his father.

I was suddenly St. Paul on the road to Damascus, struck down by the obviousness of my grandfather's dilemma. John DeWitt and his father agreed when he enlisted for the war that the younger man would be careful not to worry his mother or sisters.

I knew from my Uncle Jack, John DeWitt's son, that my grandfather was devoted to his mother and sisters. Above anything else, he would protect them and assure them he was fine. "Don't worry about me," was his way of protecting them—though I wondered if the comment had a subtext:

By the time my grandfather enlisted, his parents had already lost four sons at an early age—James, Roderick, Paul, and Raymond—a tragedy I found unimaginable as a father myself. His decision to volunteer to fight in a war in Europe must have been devastating to both his parents.

Had his father pulled him aside before he left for Camp Dodge and told him to protect his mother, to tread lightly on the things they both knew were inevitable? Had John DeWitt himself been aware of the need to distract his mother with good-natured reports after seeing his parents' sorrow at the loss of their sons?

I don't know, but as I grew to understand my grandfather through his letters, I suspect the latter.

Whatever the reason, his mother and sisters would not hear of the brutality and carnage. John DeWitt would save that part of the story for his father when he returned. The horrors he was experiencing were for later, and only for his father.

"I'll swap yarn for yarn when I get back."

I stared at that note.

In France, John DeWitt was beginning to see things so totally alien to his quiet and determined life at home that he could only take note of them and hope he survived to tell his father.

It was almost as if John Ryder DeWitt was speaking to me again, reminding me to learn more of what he went through and why he had chosen not to speak of it when he returned to Iowa.

I don't know if he shared his war stories with his father, because they never became part of our family lore. They were lost between father and son.

My desire to learn more of what he went through became more focused.

By December 1917 the Rainbow Division, including John DeWitt and the Iowa 168th, were all in France. Most, including my grandfather, might have been fervent and willing, but most were green—and they needed further training for the trench warfare that awaited.

Black Jack Pershing was well aware of the problem. He believed the war in the French trenches had reached a stalemate, with both sides bogged down in a brutal struggle in which small bits of territory were taken, then lost again in a tedious and bloody scrimmage that had thus far produced nothing but death. His end-game strategy was to use the American Expeditionary Force to push the Germans out of the trenches and defeat them through large-force maneuvers in the open.

Pershing wanted his American troops to operate independently but knew they were not ready.

It was an astute strategy, and one that would ultimately work once his troops were seasoned. That would take time. In 1917 and part of 1918, before John DeWitt was fighting, Americans were used to help French and British troops defend their lines and attack German positions. Pershing's hope for an independent American Expeditionary Force did come to fruition, beginning in May 1918, after the first American victory at Cantigny. By July 1918, French forces would begin to support the Americans.

Most of Pershing's troops, John DeWitt included, had only six months of rudimentary training before they reached France. Pershing wanted another two months of specialized instruction in France, though it became clear to me that many Americans, Merle Hay included, did not get the benefit of that necessary seasoning—which called for instruction from British and French veterans. After that, Pershing wanted his troops to have an additional month of time in "quiet sectors" before heading into battle.

The British and French soldiers who would train them, by then hardened veterans of more than two years of fighting, were not entirely convinced that Americans would offer much help.

"I do not think they had a very high opinion up to this time of the American's fighting ability for they knew we were not well trained when we began our first experience in battle," one soldier from my grandfather's own 168th, who had trained under French instructors for several weeks, recalled.

The Americans would have to prove their worth, and I'm certain John DeWitt was up to the task, likely offended by the sentiment that he was not ready. He was champing at the bit and beginning to see the realities he would soon be engulfed in.

In his December 18 letter, he also wrote:

> *We have started on our training, which will spell the defeat of the Boche before long.*

He was becoming acclimated by then.

"Boche" was a shortened version of the derogatory French description of the Germans, "cabbage head." It was common among the allied soldiers. He had an understandable reason to disparage them. By then he'd seen the damage they had caused. After re-reading what they did *was* horrible.

The Iowa 168th first taste of battle was at Badonvillers in March 1918, and its first combat deaths. Heavier fighting would come later, at Chateau Thierry, Sergy, and the Battle of the Ourq, where my grandfather and his fellow trench runners Al Boysen and Billy Shupp were in action, and Shupp was killed.

There were other deaths before then. The 168th were greeted in France by horrid weather, including bitter cold and snow. Quarters were unheated and they were hit with an outbreak of scarlet fever, meningitis, and measles that killed more than 20 men before they fired a single shot.

In France, Christmas was approaching for John DeWitt and mail was slow. His December 18 letter, the one that sparked my epiphany about his plans, was a mix of frustration and hopefulness.

I have written you three or four times previous to this and hope you receive the same. I have not heard from you since I left this time but received one written in October. I sure hope that we receive some mail before Christmas. We are experiencing a few hardships now but they are to be expected and will be the making of us in the end. We have had and are having some real experiences that will be well worth telling on our return.

It is best to figure on a month and a half from the time of sending until I receive it. Hope you have sent tobacco asked for in previous letters. Before I forget it, send me a stick of William's shaving stick and a package of Ender's blades, as we have to shave every day.

I wish you would send me as soon as possible the following: three or four pair of gloves, two or three knitted or yarn and at least one pair of leather, similar to what Dad wears, and as many pairs of the heavy socks you mentioned before as you have on hand or can get. Take real good care in the wrapping and the dressing of my packages you send to me. It is best to insure them. Wrap them in light but stout wrapping paper and be sure the writing is plain.

The next day, he was rewarded, writing:

Last night after I returned to my home, I got a lot of mail—16 letters. Three of them were from you dated the 13th, 18th and 21st of November respectively. Sure glad to hear that a bunch of "real eats" were on the way. We will probably get them just about Christmas and believe me, I can use all you can send.

Gee but it did seem good to get some mail once more.

Christmas Day, John DeWitt was elated, and clearly had enough time on his hands to write frequently. That would change, but it is clear combat was not imminent.

Merry Christmas to you one and all. This is certainly a splendid day. The sun is shining and it is just chilly. We had a snowfall of about an inch last night.

I suppose at this time you are wondering where I am and what I am doing. I am wondering what you are doing. I feel just fine and in good health.

Just got back from dinner and we had some dinner. Menu—baked turkey, dressing, potatoes, gravy, bread and butter, coffee, figs, nuts, apples and a sack of smoking tobacco. Not so bad, eh? Then better yet, I went down to the Post Office and got the box sent. Just this minute I opened it—cookies, candy and gum, candle, talcum powder, shaving stick, jar of preserves, (haven't tested them yet), handkerchiefs, tea towels, cigarettes, toothpaste, soap and gun rag.

That was sure a grand and glorious feeling when I opened that box. A couple of fellows that were with me said "your folks sure know what to put in the box". So this is a good ole Army today.

Everything is just fine with me, good health and getting lots of sleep and enough to eat so that we can work without any trouble.

I am enjoying all my experiences so don't worry about me for one little minute. You ought to know your red-headed son by this time and that he will get along alright.

Other men of the 168th were equally ebullient, caught up in the spirit of the holiday. One company hosted a Christmas celebration for a group of 400 French schoolchildren, and two American Santa Clauses handed out dolls, horns, and balloons while a local band played the *Star Spangled Banner*.

By New Year's Eve, the slow drum roll of life began picking up its cadence as the soldiers neared their mission, John Dewitt remained upbeat.

> *Happy New Year!*
>
> *Dearest Mother o' mine, Dad and those sweetest kid sisters of mine,*
>
> *I am writing this to you on the last night of a very eventful year and at the dawning of an undoubtedly more eventful year for all concerned. Without a question, it will be for me.*
>
> *I sincerely hope that you are all in the best of health and spirits at the time I am writing for I am in the best of health and spirits. I sincerely hope that the same can be said this time next year and that we will all be together again.*
>
> *I suppose that you expect to hear from me oftener but really Mother, we don't have a great deal of time to write and also there is very little of interest to write about that is not prohibited by regulations.*

In that same letter, though, took a more somber turn, mentioning the unmentionable, death—a topic he had never broached.

> *Business ought to start picking up. I witnessed a real Catholic funeral one day last week and it certainly was interesting. Altar boys carrying candles and the crucifix walking at the head, then the priest reciting Psalms and then the body in a box queer hearse and the pall bearers and mourners following on foot. The church bells ringing out across the country and against the hills and re-echoing. They certainly sound beautiful and they talked from the time the body left the house until arrival at the church and how much longer I don't know.*

He made short work of another topic, burying it in a long letter home filled with news of food packages received from home and questions about neighbors, and of course, Helen.

> *The morning was dark and snowing but went to Mass. Our bunks are too high in this barrack and I have a lower bunk on the bottom of the upper bunk. I have tacked up the picture of Dad, you and myself and the one of the girls and I and one of Helen so when I am laying down, I have you all right before my eyes.*

I was struck by a single sentence in the same letter, buried in his usual pleasantries. He did not know at the time how fateful that comment would be. He rarely spoke of it again and did not go into any detail until his long letters to my mother at college about his time in France.

He would be gassed and hospitalized in France and be awarded a Purple Heart, which my sister Abby still has in a shadow box in her home.

> *We have been issued our gas masks and steel helmets (tin hats) and there have been considerable wagers as to whether we will ever use them or not in actual combat.*

He would use both.

Large-scale use of toxic chemicals was prevalent on both sides of the war. which I wasn't aware of. The Germans would kill and cripple tens of thousands of soldiers beginning with an attack on British soldiers in 1915 at Ypres, with more than 1,100 deaths from chlorine gas asphyxiation. By the end of the war in November 1918, there were some 90,000 deaths attributed to chemical weapons.

The gas was usually placed inside an artillery shell in glass bottles, which would break and be released on impact.

As the war progressed, so too did the technology to develop chemicals that could kill large numbers of men quickly. Tear gas was merely an irritant, but chlorine, phosgene, and mustard gas were not only effective but agents of protracted and painful deaths for those who inhaled it.

Chlorine arrived in a green cloud and was thus easily identified as it approached. Phosgene, six times more lethal than chlorine, was colorless. Victims would not know they were exposed until days later, when their lungs filled with fluid and they suffocated. Mustard gas, the piece de resistance of this sordid research, was a masterpiece of killing. It would cause blisters on contact with skin, permeate uniforms, and burn through the soles of boots, rendering gas masks useless.

By the time John De Witt pulled on his mask in France for the first time, gas masks could protect soldiers from chlorine attacks. Surviving a phosgene or mustard gas attack was a matter of luck. Contemporary posters advised soldiers with such warnings as "Phosgene Smells Like Must Hay" and "Mustard Gas Smells Like Garlic."

John DeWitt's impeccable timing had once again inserted itself. Gas masks had evolved too. Earlier in the war, some men took to peeing on rags, socks, or some handy piece of cloth to protect their lungs.

He was fortunate to have an efficient gas mask. At some point in one of the letters later he says the gas mask is his best friend.

My grandfather bore no outward signs of his own encounters with gas after he returned to Iowa.

The 168th was not immune to the attacks. In May 1918, more than 400 were gassed and forty-seven were killed. An honor roll recalled the deaths of two men in my grandfather's own Company L from Council Bluffs. Surely, he must have known them. He made no mention of them in his letters home, just as he made no mention of his fellow trench runners from Council Bluffs, Billy Shupp and Al Boysen.

John W. Price of Council Bluffs "fought bravely against great odds to overcome the gas that he inhaled in the gas attack on Village Negre. He quietly obeyed all instructions, but died in the hospital in Baccarat."

William A. Staley, also of Council Bluffs, "did not recover from the shock of the tremendous explosion in the gas attack in time to get his mask on and died a short time later. Private Staley died as he became an American soldier, enduring his suffering without a word."

All that lay ahead for John DeWitt. As the holidays ended, he continued being the generous soldier without an apparent care in the world.

> *I have gotten more good use and enjoyment from those bed socks than anything else I have with me. They have kept my feet warm more than once than they perhaps would have been cold. Tom Hanson's barrack was lost on the way from* [censored] *to here and the poor kid*

was without everything except what he had on his back or in his pack so I let him have one pair and he has been making use of them ever since. The knitted goods have helped a great deal towards making me comfortable in spite of conditions.

I had another jolt in my quest to learn more of the mysterious Helen, whom my grandfather mentioned frequently. I learned why in his Christmas letter.

Well it is almost time to go to bed, that is one thing we certainly get enough of over in this country, sleep. I want to write Helen a short note tonight without fail because a year ago tonight we had some experiences and a swell time.

The boy was lovestruck!

Soon enough, as the new year began, he'd have things other than Helen to occupy himself. Some long, hard slogs were ahead, and this time they would not be in the safety and warmth of Camp Dodge or in front of adoring crowds at Camp Mills.

ELEVEN

MONTHS INTO MY search an amazing thing began to unfold as I slowly re-read my grandfather's letters. Caught up in the easy banter of his notes, I began to hear the familiar voice of the old man I'd visited in Griswold, Iowa as a kid. I could almost detect the thick aroma of his cigars. I found that phenomenon comforting.

By then, familiar with the entire set of letters my sister had found, I realized my grandfather's notes home were like the North Atlantic icebergs he and his fellow soldiers dodged on their way to France in November 1917.

Beneath the surface of his chatty notes home was a more important story, not just about my grandfather, but about an entire generation of young men now for the most part forgotten.

I also made an important discovery that dissolved any exasperation I felt over his reluctance to share details. Once I began to tie the dates of his letters to what was happening in France, I learned what he was going through. I did not now need him to fill in the blanks.

Along the way I discovered something else. On the verge of the inevitable combat he had volunteered and trained for, and despite his dearth of introspection, my grandfather's light-hearted letters were ample evidence of a strong, unstated courage. Courage—a stoic control of his fears—was his touchstone. He needed to show courage not only to his father when he returned home, but to himself as he waged war.

His insistence to his mother and sisters that "all was well" was more than an attempt to protect them. He genuinely felt that all was well. He was not worried, and he was not putting up a front.

In the midst of brutal combat, running trenches under heavy fire and dodging German snipers, he was just fine.

It was the same quiet confidence I'd recognize in my old Grampa as we talked decades later.

IN LATE November, the three largest regiments of the Rainbow Division—from Ohio, Alabama and New York—settled into villages around division headquarters at Vancouleurs, in Lorraine. Some 150 miles east of Paris, Vancouleurs was the village where Joan of Arc began her crusade, though I'm not sure if it was chosen for its symbolism or location. The 168th Iowa, after the delays caused by the problems with the *US Grant,* would join them on December 12, settling in Rimacourt some 30 miles away.

These billets were temporary, a brief respite for the soldiers to continue training and hope that the thinly stretched supply lines prompted by the rapid mobilization that began in April would have time to strengthen.

The men were still playing at war, rehearsing for what lay ahead and getting the additional training Black Jack Pershing knew was necessary. The men drilled with artillery, took target practice with machine-guns, rifles, pistols, and trench-mortars. They did bayonet and gas drills. They dug trenches and built shelters. They studied maneuvers and terrain problems and practiced throwing grenades. And, of course, they marched.

The steady flow of letters from my grandfather after he reached France were ample evidence that, at first, he still had a fair amount of spare time to continue writing home. Things would change quickly after the holidays. With the relative peace and comfort of Christmas and New Year's Day behind him, my usually prolific grandfather stopped his almost daily stream of letters home for nearly three weeks.

He would enclose three letters in a single envelope and send them home after February 8. Dated January 26, and February 7 and 8, none said where he was, but the Rainbow division was heading north on foot.

The idealistic young man from Council Bluffs who had enlisted eight months before was heading to war. By early March the drills were over, and any further training lessons would be instilled in real life-and-death situations.

Letter-writing became, at least for a short while, a superfluous luxury.

He was busy with other things, I would learn, one of which was an arduous 60-mile hike in horrid conditions to the village of Rolampont, where the U.S. Army's new training had been established.

That march was just the beginning. John De Witt and the rest of the 168th had little time to do much of anything but get into position to begin fighting, and that meant long slogs in demanding weather. The grueling treks drained energy for doing anything else but marching, resting as much as one could, then marching again.

In all three letters, my grandfather was excitedly grateful for food and gifts and tobacco received, full of questions about home, and, as always, filled with his assurances of his unfailingly good health. He avoided any details about what he was going through.

He was a master of selective information.

He was heading for the front when he wrote those, I knew. He was no longer writing of parades at Camp Mills, the excitement of New York City, his passage across the Atlantic, or the sights of England.

I was struck by his growing proficiency for avoiding the obvious—impressed by the creativity and effort he put into writing entertaining and engaging letters home without saying anything about what was going on.

By the time he was marching to the front in France, he had seen fellow soldiers die, heard the cacophony of artillery, and suffered from scarcity of food and proper winter clothing as the thinly stretched Rainbow Division waited for supplies to catch up.

My grandfather was becoming a master of evasion, a letter-writing maestro of a form that was not so much fiction as it was smoke and mirrors. His letters remained entertaining, but his ability to distract became finely tuned.

> *January 26, 1918*
> *Somewhere in France*
>
> *I received a swell toilet case from [MESCO], toothbrush and paste, comb, mirror, wash rag and rubber case, razor, shaving brush, soapbox and soap. I finally got Helen's box with a wristwatch, carton of cigarettes, 2 pound box of candy and some nuts. The wristwatch is something I have been wanting badly for quite a while. I got a box of mighty fine homemade candy. It was a real treat.*

On February 8, as the Iowa 168th made its way to its first battle at Lunenberg, he wrote his *piece de resistance*, a startlingly ironic and masterful sentence of obfuscation.

France is certainly a very beautiful country.

My God, I thought to myself as I read that. If one put aside the ravaged villages my grandfather had passed through, and the ruined farms and innocent civilians killed, I suppose France would be a beautiful country. But that was his imagined pastoral and idyllic France before the war. Grampa was conjuring an image he knew his parents wanted to hear, and he gave it to them.

I did know one thing about that curious sentence that was startlingly true. By February 8, 1918, John Dewitt had seen enough of the country to pass judgement on what it once must have looked like. He had slogged slowly through it, carrying a heavy pack, one foot after the other as he marched with his ragged formation to the front.

According to the 1919 book *The Story of the Rainbow Division,* the 60-mile march to Rolampont in a blizzard was an effort that "any man who made it with his two feet will never forget."

The Rainbow Division soldiers who marched to Rolampont would soon remember the trek as "The Valley Forge Hike."

"They made most of the hike on sheer grit. Great drifts piled up under the sweeping winds, and in some places the snow lay flat three or four feet deep. The men were not hardened to long hikes even under fair conditions; they had not entirely straightened out the kinks of the cramping ocean trip.

Their shoes wore out—men were marching barefooted through the snow sometimes; they wrapped bags around their feet and kept on. There were bloody tracks along the route of the column."

If the below-zero temperatures were not enough of a deterrent, mumps and pneumonia broke out and spread quickly. There were not enough ambulances to carry the men to hospitals. In one regiment, five hundred men simply stopped, unable to carry on.

The reward for withstanding the ardors of the Valley Forge Hike was further training at Rolampont, and more such hikes into the trenches and combat.

The Story of the Rainbow Division described the arrival at Rolampont:

"As the division thawed out and got clothes and shoes and fighting equipment, its confidence grew. The future was shaping up now, growing plainer; there was fighting ahead, that was certain, but they wanted to fight. They were eager to get up there on the line."

On February 7, my grandfather wrote with great pride of how he handled one such hike. It was the closest I had seen him come to crowing about himself.

Bragging was unusual, but he was in an unusual situation.

> *Quite a bit of time has elapsed since I first started this letter but a great many things have happened since then. I went on police duty for two days, then we had to pack our stuff and more. We are in a small French village now. We established a new record on hike from there to here. It is a little better than 40 miles. They contemplated on taking three days but we made it in two. When you stop to consider that we made it with full equipment, weighing close to 70 pounds, it was some feat. Very few of us fellows fell out the first day and only one the second. It was sure a test of endurance.*

I know I had to use every bit of reserve and I had to make it and it was the same with practically the entire company. The honor of the company carried a big bunch of the fellows through that would not have made it otherwise.

On February 15, 1918, orders arrived to go to the front. The preliminaries were over. For the Rainbow Division the war was about to begin. On February 16 the division began to roll northward, toward the Luneville Sector in Lorraine. The smell of battle wafted nearby, but my grandfather would only hint at it.

I am just fine, as usual, and even feeling better than usual. This has been a grand ole Army lately. The food has been fine and so has everything else besides business is going to pick up very soon and that is what we have been waiting for.

"Business" would indeed "pick up."

He followed up with an undated letter, likely three or four days later.

I think I told in my last letter that we were going to move. Well we did and it was strenuous moving. We marched about 8 miles to the railroad point and trained in box cars. Capacity—40 men or 18 horses. Rode all that night until 12:30 that day, unloaded and did a lot of work, marched over 10 miles to this village, didn't get here until about 8:30 that night. By the time we got straightened out and had supper, it was 10:30, a nice day's work.

We are much nearer the front now and, in fact, we can hear the big guns without any trouble. On our way

> *here, we passed through village after village, the greater part of them—nothing but ruins. Yes, I have seen some things and witnessed many others that I have often seen pictures of and read about but there is nothing like seeing the real thing.*

By February 21, the men of the Iowa 168th were close to the front lines of a battle that would last until March 23, with the Allies emerging victorious. The Germans had launched what would be their last major offensive just as the men of the 168th were ready to fight. It was perhaps the first time John DeWitt's run of good timing and good luck hit a bump. The 168th Infantry Regiment was the first American unit to take control over the Baccarat sector from the French Army, evidence that Pershing's plan for an independent American effort was gelling.

The men from Camp Dodge had their first taste of combat on March 5, a brutal day in which nineteen soldiers were killed and another thirty-eight wounded during a German artillery bombardment.

The dead included Captain Harrison Cummins McHenry of Des Moines, the first Iowa officer to die. Cummins, from a prominent Des Moines family, had been a two-sport star at Drake University and his obituary in the *Des Moines Register* called him "an ideal soldier, physically, mentally and morally." His death was front page news and a quote from a letter to his mother was later used in a war bond fund-raising effort.

"I will try to be a credit to you. I will never be a coward to bring disgrace to you. Good-bye, mother, God keep you safe."

Germans began bombarding American lines at 4:30 that morning, shelling all four sides of the 168th's position encampment, trying to cut the men off from reinforcements and to sever its communications.

As one platoon rushed to its mortar placements to respond, a German howitzer shell exploded near the base of the mortar, killing seven men instantly, three of whom were vaporized, with no identifiable body parts ever found.

Captain McHenry, who had left his command position to order the launch of a mortar rocket, was killed in the same explosion.

The German bombardment lasted for more than one and a half hours, but the 168th prevailed and the enemy was repulsed.

It would be my grandfather's first total immersion in combat, though he had certainly seen much by then.

> *March 9*
>
> *Everything is still fine and dandy. We are still all okay. We are right up where things are doing. "where things are doing". It is sure interesting and noisy. I suppose you know by this time that our regiment was in the thick of things and that we lost a few. The Iowa boys have sure acquitted themselves with honor so far.*
>
> *There has been a lot doing today and it is still going on. Just came back from up on the hill where we have been watching the flash of rockets and etc.*

Life went on. John DeWitt was still himself. "Interesting and noisy" was as detailed as he cared to go.

Ahead lay the trenches and his new challenge as a runner.

TWELVE

AMERICAN SOLDIERS IN France reading the April 5, 1918, edition of *The Stars and Stripes*—which meant just about everyone—were greeted with a message from President Woodrow Wilson.

Running across the top of the newspaper's front page, Wilson's short note thanked the troops on the first anniversary of American involvement in the war.

> *Please convey to the officers and men in our Expeditionary Force my warmest greetings on this the anniversary of the entrance of the United States into this great war for Liberty, and to say to them that we all not only have greatly admired and been very proud of the way they have so far accounted for themselves, but have the utmost confidence that in every test they will prove to be made of the finest mettle of free men.*

It had been a month since my grandfather and the Iowa 168th Infantry mourned their dead after watching the Germans retreat into the rolling hills around Luneville.

In the mud in France, John DeWitt had just finished a remarkable and tumultuous twelve months.

In April 1917 he had been traveling the back roads of Iowa and Nebraska as a salesman, trying to figure out a way to afford medical school. Then, the three-year-old war in Europe held little interest for most Americans, including the leaders of its small and under-equipped army and navy.

A year later, my grandfather was a trained and hardened soldier who by St. Patrick's Day had begun running messages under fire between command posts buried in the labyrinth of muddy trenches stretching across Western France.

The victory at Luneville, small but significant, illustrated something the men from the Rainbow Division seemed to know from the beginning. It showed, as one observer noted "the American doughboy could lick the Boche."

The Americans, still green and untested, were confident and self-assured to the point that, of course, they knew the Germans would retreat once they faced American might—Wilson's "finest mettle of free men."

Beating the Germans and ending a war that was nearly four years old was why they had trained and had endured the long slog to Europe in U-boat-infested waters. By the war's end in November, they would suffer horrible losses, watch friends die, and live in the ugliness of the trenches—but they would prevail.

My grandfather was impatient to get into the fight. On March 1 he had written home:

> *Didn't drill this afternoon so we had a lot of fun but we would almost just as soon drill. The fellows feel that the more we drill, the better we will be when we meet the damn Germans.*

He and the rest of his "fellows" would soon meet the damn Germans and send them running. Reading my grandfather's letters and contemporary accounts of battles, I began to sense a certain amount of cockiness in the Americans as they began fighting.

That same March 1 note home to his mother also provided a clue to my grandfather's mindset, why he was willing to step up and start fighting. The Americans were on a righteous mission to protect the innocent.

> *Evidence all around us at the cruelty of the Germans. There are 2 little girls here that have had their eyesight ruined by the Germans.*

Righteous or not, the war my grandfather was now fully involved in was a war that would take the lives of millions of civilian victims. Innocent bystanders would die from malnutrition and famine, forced resettlement, epidemics, and bombing. No other war to that point would kill more people because the technology of war had become more efficient than ever, with tanks, airplanes, submarines, machine guns, modern artillery, flamethrowers, and poison gas.

As I immersed myself in my grandfather's letters, I grew certain he spent little or no time contemplating the meaning of life and the strange events that had brought him to the squalid trenches in France, under fire. Grampa was a pragmatist. He was there to do a job he'd volunteered for, finish it, and get home and move on with his life.

I'm certain he had already thought it out, envisioned his future back in Iowa. I'm sure he did not think overly long about getting killed. He would return home, proud of doing his part and knowing he had never flinched. He would figure out a way to afford medical school or find another reputable career where he could use his mind and intellect. I think, too, that he planned to marry the Helen he wrote so often and affectionately about to his mother.

Americans saw the Germans as brutal—and saw themselves as saviors. My grandfather's letters were clear about that. I have no doubt that my grandfather's first taste of combat neither rattled him nor gave him pause to wax philosophically about his fate, even as he watched his comrades die outside Luneville. He was focused and undeterred, as were most of the Americans he served with. They had forced the Germans to retreat, and I sensed from the matter-of-fact tone of my grandfather's letters, he was neither surprised nor overly elated about the results.

On March 9, he would tell his mother:

> *All I want at present is to get in some of that action work against the damn Germans.*

That is what all the Americans wanted to do, and they did it well. At Luneville the Americans brought their own style and their own way of doing things.

From the beginning, it seemed the Americans would fight differently than did the British and French, who followed odd and seemingly oxymoronic customs about fairness and good sport in combat.

In the area around Luneville, the German attackers and French defenders had agreed to spare the surrounding villages from the ravages of war, and to eschew the use of toxic gas. The antagonists rarely fought during daylight.

Customs were so entrenched that German soldiers would emerge from their trenches to do their laundry in water-filled shell holes while French troops watched from theirs. The arrival of the Americans would change that. Taking a position over No Man's Land, Americans fired at the Germans doing their wash, to the great annoyance of French officers.

The Americans brought attitude.

One of the newly arrived Americans is reported to have said, "What the hell?" I came out here to kill Germans, not to sit here and watch them wash clothes."

Even the press coverage contained a bit of swagger. The same edition of *The Stars and Stripes* that offered President Wilson's anniversary note contained an account of a bold American patrol, its mission, and the inevitable defeat of fleeing Germans.

A.E.F. PATROLS MAKE DAYLIGHT CALLS ON HUNS
THIRTY FLEE BEFORE FIVE

> *They're a shameless bunch, these Americans. They'd just as soon stroll around No Man's Land in daylight as at night. What's more, they've done it twice lately, and they've gotten away with it both times.*
>
> *The article recounted how an American sergeant the three privates wasted no time in volunteering to head out to look for prisoners, even though dawn was approaching. The Americans were serious about their business, heading out after hearing that six Germans had been spotted in an outpost in No Man's Land.*
>
> *Confronted, four Germans surrendered immediately. Two others began to run as the American shouted "halt."*
>
> *The Boches paid no heed. The Americans did not call again. They fired and the two refractory Boshes dropped in their tracks.*

Sitting at my desk in front of a stack of his letters more than 100 years after he fought in France, I tried to put my finger on my grandfather's state of mind and motivations.

He was not a cocky man. As a kid and a teen, I'd never seen a single incident of him being arrogant or full of himself. I had never seen him be anything but my quiet Grampa. Nor had I heard family members or friends complain about his ego. John Dewitt was quietly confident but not a braggart or know-it-all. It was not in his genes.

But he was a proud man, not one to sit back if he saw something that offended him. In his letters home he had disparaged the slackers at Camp Mills. I don't doubt he thought very little of the men in France who were reluctant to fight.

He was not yellow, as he told his father, and never would be.

What drove him? He was supremely confident in his purpose and his mission, I finally decided. I know too that he was comforted by his Catholicism and his regular participation in the rites—Mass and communion and confession—that promised him eternal life.

During the war he had done what was necessary to not merely survive but to beat the staggering odds that said he'd be killed quickly when he became a runner.

He was driven only by a determination to rid the world of evil and perhaps test himself and his courage. He was champing at the bit and ready.

In his first battle things had gotten a little "interesting and noisy" but the Americans won, and they won their way. The Germans had rushed the American trenches and they paid a price for it. As the Germans retreated, the No Man's Land between trenches was littered with their bodies, many hanging over the barbed wire they had tried to break through.

On March 9, 1918, assisted by the French, Rainbow Division artillery and machine guns softened German lines for an all-out attack by American and French soldiers who left the safety of their trenches—"going over the top," as it became known.

The assaulting force destroyed German shelters and captured prisoners. None other than Colonel Douglas

MacArthur, the division's chief of staff, had been among the attackers, leaving the trench in a regular soldier's uniform and capturing a German himself.

On March 17, St. Patrick's Day, two officers and 50 men from New York's 165th Infantry destroyed a German stronghold, taking control of a trench and holding it. Four New Yorkers were killed, three wounded, and one reported as missing.

It was a first for American troops in the war.

John DeWitt was not one to let St. Patrick's Day pass without writing home and making note of it.

Of course, he told his mother he was fine, in great spirits, and as always, hungry. And of course, he mentioned Helen and church:

> *March 17, 1918*
> *Somewhere in France*
>
> *Dearest Mother o' mine,*
>
> *Hurrah for St. Patrick!! France is no place for an Irishman on this day of all days but here I am! In the best of health and spirits and feeling oh so fine.*
>
> *I got a very nice box from Helen F. with a lot of eats. I was sure surprised on receiving a box from the Messco boys and girls containing tobacco, cigarettes, fruitcake, candy and the book. Things like that sure help.*
>
> *Today is also Sunday and no opportunity to go to church but that must be expected here. We certainly have had beautiful weather here for the last month or so.*

By then, weeks into fighting, things had changed radically for my grandfather. He mentions for the first time his new job as a "battalion runner."

> *I will be able to write some real interesting letters before long. We are in the trenches at present, have been for a while and will be for a while longer. Things sure happen around this place and this is a lively evening. I just got back from a run and it was sure noisy.*
>
> *Conditions are much better here than we expected. I was fortunate in getting assigned as Battalion Runner. Will explain more later.*

He remained defiant. That would never change.

I pictured him under fire, in the mud, writing away calmly.

> *As I sit here, I can hear the roar of our guns sending a few "kisses" to Fritzie and I can hear his kisses exploding also. This is the life. Gee but it is hard to write a letter.*

THIRTEEN

ITS FIRST TASTE of battle and the elation of victory left the soldiers of the Rainbow Division and the 168th Iowa confident of their mission. Morale could not have been higher.

The 168th Iowa had sent the Germans running. After Luneville, the American boys did not sit back and relish their success. They took charge and became the aggressors.

By mid-March, the Rainbow Division had been holding a front-line sector for almost a month and was ordered back to Rolampont for a rest. The respite was short-lived. The Iowa 168th was ordered back to the trenches and the front—and with few exceptions would be on the move for the rest of the war.

A last-gasp German offensive had begun by March 21 and according to *The History of the Rainbow Division,* "for two days every German gun from the North Sea to the Swiss border had fired steadily on towns, roads, batteries, posts of command."

By the war's end the 168th would figure heavily in battles at Champagne-Marne, Aisne-Marne, St. Mihiel, Meuse-Argonne, Lorraine, and Champagne.

John DeWitt would see much carnage, but in his letters, he had come up with a new term to avoid discussing anything untoward that was going on. As my grandfather saw it, everything was "fine and dandy"—an expression that appeared in many of his letters home.

By this point in my research, I knew things were anything but fine and dandy.

I found myself returning to my grandfather's St. Patrick's Day letter to his mother. As always, it was upbeat, even as his colleagues were being killed.

His casual references to death made me catch my breath. Had he shut his emotions off and become hardened once the guns began firing? Or was he simply dealing with the reality in his own way?

> *I suppose you have heard of the deaths in our regiment? Such is war. One of the kids was a real good friend of mine, although he wasn't in our Company.*

"Such is war" seemed to me a worn cliché, callous and not something I could picture my grandfather saying. For the men of the 168th, the war was no longer abstract. It surrounded them.

In his St. Patrick's Day letter, a Sunday in 1918, my grandfather had written that there was "no opportunity to go to church but that must be expected here."

The men of the 168th had other things to do that day, taking the initiative to go after the Germans in what became known as "The St. Patrick's Day Raid."

During skirmishes earlier in March with the Germans, men from the 168th noticed that the enemy had been busy building fortifications along their lines. A party of seventeen men from K Company and eight men from I Company took it on themselves to destroy the German's new work.

According to *The Story of the 168th,* a large number of these 25 men were of Irish descent. I have no doubt Grampa would have loved to have jumped at the chance to join in a fight with the Boche on such an auspicious day—even if it meant missing Mass.

The Iowans would creep into No Man's Land under protective artillery fire and destroy seven recently built German dugouts with grenades and incendiary bombs.

According to *The Story of the 168thy Infantry by* John Huddleston Taber, a young officer who served throughout the war, "one anxious youth, whose intentions were better than his aim, tossed a bomb at a dugout mouth, but it missed the mark and, glancing off the side, fell at the feet of Lieutenant Cotter. In a second the air was thick with blazing bits of phosphorus, and before he knew it the lieutenant's breeches were on fire. The situation was desperate, as there were no barrels [WATER] available, but by a concerted effort the conflagration was extinguished before any irremediable harm was done."

The mission was no lark. Three men from K Company were wounded and another killed.

On March 21, the 168th was at it again. A patrol crossed into a wooded No Man's Land in a drizzling rain, marching in single file, behind a French contingent.

"The Huns knew just where our men were, but the Americans could only guess at the position of the enemy from the flashes of their guns. It was pitch black, and the heavy atmosphere held the smoke in a solid blanket, so that in a few moments it was impossible to see either friend or foe," John Taber wrote.

They met the Germans in a raucous firefight, from which the Germans withdrew. One American had several fingers blown off by a German grenade. A second man, Edward

Monahan of Sioux City was hit by a grenade and machine gun fire, which shattered his leg and broke his arm.

Taber related the scene:

> *Although mortally wounded and fully conscious of his condition, Monahan refused to be considered out of the scrap. As he lay in the bottom of the trench, he encouraged the men fighting above him. "If they get too strong for you", he said, "give me some grenades—my right arm is still good." Later, while being carried back on a stretcher, he jollied the stretcher-bearers, as if to divert their minds from his suffering.*
>
> *"Hip-te-diddy, it's a grand old life if you don't weaken," he smilingly informed them.*

He would die ten days later.

My grandfather was seeing much of that and what he had seen would have been reason enough for him to become increasingly calloused, or perhaps more accurately, numb. But he never did.

Such is war indeed, I thought.

It is quite clear to me that though they were quickly gaining combat experience, the men of the 168th were hardly battle-seasoned veterans. It was still early days for them, including my grandfather.

According to Taber, who had served with the men since Camp Dodge, during the first month of combat in France the 168th "learned more about the rough-and-ready practical conduct of war than two years of drill and practice and study behind the lines could have given it."

Central to the firefights and skirmishes with the Germans and the constant bombardments as the Iowans immersed themselves in the war were the trenches.

FOURTEEN

ALWAYS, THERE WERE the trenches.

Considering he spent untold hours in the trenches, my grandfather rarely mentioned them in his letters home, and never described them. I'd learn that it was for good reason. While "trenches" had a connotation of neatness and shelter—some basic form of protection—life in the trenches was complicated, and above everything else, overwhelmingly unpleasant.

There was no way for Grampa to describe his daily life without at least mentioning the trenches, but that was as far as he'd go. He spared his parents and sisters the grimmer details though.

And "grim" I would learn, was too polite a word to describe life there.

On St. Patrick's Day, he wrote:

> *We are in the trenches at present, have been for a while and will be for a while longer. Things sure happen around this place and this is a lively evening. I just got back from a run and it was sure noisy.*

A week later, on March 26:

> *We are out of the trenches for a rest and then back we go for a longer period.*

On April 3:

> *Everything is fine and dandy, although instead of getting that rest I told you about in my last letter, why we are back close to the trenches again and expect to be in them again before long. This is going to be a much longer spell than the last one too.*

At first glance, one would think life in the trenches offered at least a vague sense of comfort and perhaps even safety from German fire. Soldiers would always head to the trenches after a battle or skirmish. It seemed to me that the refuge offered by the trenches came at great cost. I would learn the reality of life there was a nightmarish stew of disease, stench, discomfort, and danger.

Trenches served strategically as company headquarters and communications posts. Their deep walls offering at least some scant protection. Soldiers slept, ate, cleaned themselves as much as possible, relieved themselves, relaxed as much as possible. They passed their quieter moments there, chatted with buddies, commiserated about their circumstances, and in many cases, sat on makeshift bunks and wrote letters home when they had a chance.

While he never wrote to his family singing the praises of trench life, my grandfather also avoided details of how truly putrid the trenches were.

For good reason, I soon realized.

In many instances the trenches were more dangerous than the battles themselves.

John Taber wrote chillingly of one unfortunate soldier who died because he was unfamiliar with the "labyrinthic turnings and branchings of the trench system."

"They all look alike, and one seldom sees them in perspective, or is able to orient himself by observation; at night it is worse," Tabor said.

Private Harry J. Clarke of the 168th became ill and was ordered to report to the infirmary in a nearby town. A doctor pronounced Clarke ill enough to check into the company hospital and sent him back to his post in the trenches to collect his gear.

Clarke apparently became disoriented and wandered into an abandoned trench, where he was killed by a German shell. Search parties were eventually sent to look for Clarke but "he seemed to have mysteriously disappeared, for not a trace of him could be found."

Clarke's mud-covered body was found two weeks later in a trench by engineers repairing wire at the edge of No Man's Land. The man who discovered Clarke's body at first thought it was a sandbag.

Unlike my grandfather, another Iowan was happy to share his trench experience with others. Hugh S. Thompson, a lieutenant in the 168th, wrote an account of a tour he made that was at first serialized in newspapers and later appeared in his book, *Trench Knives and Mustard Gas: With the 42nd Rainbow Division in France.*

> *We left the clearing, skidded down a steep communicating trench, and crossed a low place. A bullet pinged overhead. Three shells swished over us in rapid succession and exploded in the direction of Badonviller. I began to get a bit uncomfortable over what was in store for us. Floundering through mud, we crossed a brook, passed another rustic grave, and pulled up in front of a chicken-wire gate. A sentinel admitted us into another trench.*

We splashed by a muddy group that worked with shovels in the trench bottom. Floundering around a corner, we came to a dugout and adjoining shelter, covered with sunken hoods of corrugated iron. A doughboy stood by the blanketed entrance to the dugout. Another, with rifle and bayonet, lay on his belly upon a pile of mud atop. We were at the platoon headquarters. Wallace led us around a bayou and into a fire trench. The sight that greeted us brought an immediate and positive reaction. "Desolate" was the only name for it. A mass of rusty barbed wire was strung on crisscrosses of posts that seemed to grow from the ground. Ghost-like trees to the right were splattered with shell scars. Some had fallen into the mass of twisted wire and upturned earth. Others were broken off at various heights, like so many matchsticks. The expanse of desolation sloped up a gentle rise. The German trenches were hidden behind the crest some two hundred yards or more away.

We retraced our difficult steps, following our guide to the neighboring platoon positions. We lurched down soupy, demolished trenches toward GC 10. Men in rubber boots, hip high, grunted with shovels, here and there. Others worked in the tangles of mud, splintered stanchions, broken telephone cable, and twisted iron. A Boche plane buzzed overhead as we approached a dark cavity in the earth filled with splintered debris.

Doughboys with automatic rifles were in outposts jutting out along the line. Two men sat at each gun, while another pair slept under metal and sandbag shelters, close at hand. A heavily manned outpost between GC 10 and GC11 had its gun set up among the ruins of a farmhouse

> *with the muzzle stuck through a wide slit in a tumbled-down chimney. More men slept in a waterlogged cellar below. A German helmet hung from a spike in the chimney's mortar, raw flesh and tufts of black hair protruding from the lining.*
>
> *Wallace took us into GC it, which was out of his company sector. He had a special reason. We were greeted by a sickening odor, as he led us around a turn in a sloppy ditch. The body of a dead German, in muddy, green-gray overcoat lay on the trench bottom.*

Both the Germans and Allies used trenches as a defensive military tactic. Trenches offered protection from artillery bombardments and prevented enemy troops from advancing. Historians now agree the systems served to prolong the war.

Those same historians and recollections from soldiers who lived in the trenches unanimously agree that daily life was nightmarish. If it rained, and it rained often in the spring of 1918, trenches would flood. Walls would collapse. The resulting mud would make passages unnavigable—to the point that soldiers would become trapped and, in some cases, drown.

I found the engineering basics of trenches fascinating.

On the Western Front, at the beginning of the war, trenches were little more than shallow dugouts that offered a small measure of protection. As the war and the stalemate between the Germans and Allied troops continued, trenches became more elaborate. By the end of 1914, trench systems on the Western Front were roughly 475 miles long, stretching from the French coast on the English Channel to the Swiss Alps—close to the distance from Cleveland to New York City.

As the construction of the trenches became more sophisticated, the sandbag-lined trenches were constructed in a zigzag pattern, so if an enemy entered the trenches, he could not fire in a straight line. As further precaution, soldiers used periscopes and mirrors to see above the sandbags. Walls could easily collapse from frequent shelling or steady rainfall. Some trenches could be as deep as 20 or 30 feet.

Engineering basics and clever construction do not tell the tale of the lives of the men, John DeWitt included, who lived within the trenches. John DeWitt's trench life was appalling.

Tabor described the sanitary conditions of the trenches when the 168th took them over as "deplorable." Trenches were claustrophobic, stagnant and at the mercy of the dank weather. Illnesses, including trench foot, trench fever, and dysentery were rife because soldiers lived among piles of filth and bodily waste, with scant supplies of safe water to drink. Soldiers would often have to resort to drinking water from shell holes. Decomposing bodies awaiting burial created an ideal breeding ground for rats.

I could not imagine my grandfather relating any of these grim facts to his parents and sisters at home in Council Bluffs. Nor for that matter, could I envision the older man I knew sitting me on his knee and relating stories of rats and bodies.

I did notice that trench life did not dampen my Grampa's appetite. The man could eat—and nothing would deter him, even the paltry food available to the soldiers. Meals, not surprisingly, were often cold and possibly contaminated. The logistics of bringing food to soldiers often under fire were daunting, but the Americans under Black Jack Pershing were determined to give its soldiers ample nutrition to carry on.

American quartermasters tried to give soldiers three basic supplies of food.

When food prepared in field kitchens could not be delivered, hungry soldiers had choices. In their backpacks they might have a "field ration" that included canned meat, dried bread, coffee, and salt. Or they could be offered a "trench ration" of corned beef, sardines, salmon, salt, sugar and cigarettes—a vice my grandfather enjoyed.

As a last resort, soldiers might get an "emergency ration" of high-calorie food such as chocolate.

Whatever the food offered by the Army was, it was literally not "something to write home about."

While my grandfather in his earlier letters often waxed poetic about the wonderful meals he had been served. Once he got into combat, he never mentioned his meals in the trenches.

Instead he wrote home effusively, mentioning packages of food he'd gratefully received.

On March 9 he would write:

> *I got a nice big package from Helen F. today and it had a lot of eats and Camels in it.*

In his long St, Patrick's Day letter he wrote:

> *I got a very nice box from Helen F. with a lot of eats. I was sure surprised on receiving a box from the Messco boys and girls containing tobacco, cigarettes, fruitcake, candy and the book. Things like that sure help.*

I was astounded by a passage in his March 26 note home.

> *I hope you have not been worrying about me. I am all okay and no worries.*

> *Tell Dad I think I have picked up weight but haven't had a chance to weigh myself.*
>
> *Best you don't stop sending me eats but keep them coming! Send another cake in a tin.*

In the middle of combat, in the depths and stench of the trenches, John Ryder DeWitt was gaining weight.

I was awestruck.

He only made me admire him more in his letter of April 3, which provided a clue about his prodigious appetite.

> *Gee, don't know anything else to write. It gets harder to write every time. Went into town about a week ago and ate a dozen eggs along with a lot of bread and butter and jam and coffee. The next day I ate a half dozen for dinner.*

Such is war, I thought.

John Dewitt in his uniform, age 21

The DeWitt house, 1977

John DeWitt's mother Agnes Ryder DeWitt. Without her saving the letters from her son this book would not be possible

John DeWitt as a Griswold, Iowa attorney

Agnes Ryder DeWitt and her son John

John, Helen, Maribeth, and Jack DeWitt

AMERICAN EXPEDITIONARY FORCES
26 July, 1918.

From; Asst. Division Adjutant, 42d Division,
To: Pvt. John DeWitt, Co. L, 168th Infantry, (through Military channels),
Subject: Commendation.

I am directed by the Division Commander to inform you that your conduct on the occasion of the bombardment northeast of SUIPPES July 15, 1918, when you carried important messages to your company commander at a time the trenches were shelled so violently you were compelled to take the exposed route over the top and although being slightly gassed you insisted upon staying on duty, has been brought to his personal attention and he considers your performance of duty on this occasion worthy of the highest commendation. He regards your actions, in the face of the enemy, gallant, an example to your comrades in arms and characteristic of that splendid standard upon which the traditions of our military establishment are founded.

James E. Thomas,
Captain, N.G., Adjutant General.

h

1st Ind.

Hq. 168th Inf. A.E.F. 7 Aug 1918. To: Pvt. John Dewitt, Co. L, 168th Inf. (Thru C. O. Co. L, 168th Inf.)

P.I.V.

OGM

Letter of commendation for John DeWitt for his actions on the day he was gassed and injured ending his active duty

John DeWitt's Purple Heart for injuries obtained July 18, 1918

This was also the time of the Spanish flu of 1918
which killed millions of people across the world

John and Helen DeWitt and the author's mother, Maribeth DeWitt Chase

John DeWitt's High School graduation picture

Author's mother and her husband Jack Chase visiting John DeWitt who was bedridden on their wedding day due to a fractured spine in an auto accident.

From left to right: John, Helen, Maribeth and Jack DeWitt

John and Helen DeWitt with their grandchildren.
Bottom to top: Kit, Claire, and the author.

Parade given to send off the American troops to Europe

John DeWitt reading final tribute to a fallen comrade

INSTRUCTIONS FOR TROOPS

YOUR BUNK NO. IS	DECK NO. 4	COMPT. NO. D	BUNK 73

Decks are numbered from main deck down.
Compartments are lettered from bow to stern.
See blue-prints on bulletin boards.

GENERAL MESS DIRECTIONS

1. When mess-gear is sounded every man will go to his assigned bunk and stand by with his mess-kit.
2. There will be three shifts to mess. Each compartment will answer the same call for every meal. Wait in your berthing compartment until your call sounds.
3. Follow specific mess directions posted in your berthing compartment and use only the ladders directed to mess-space.
4. Keep in single file to serving tables. Wash your gear and get out of mess compartment up on deck as quickly as possible.
5. Stay up on deck until call sounds to go below to stow mess-kits.
6. Mess shifts as follows:--
   First Call.---Men in compartments 3C, 4C, 3G and 2J.
   Second Call---Men in compartments 3B, 4B, 3D, 4G and 3J.
   Third Call---Men in compartments 4D, 3H, 4H and 4J.

Non-Commissioned Officers will mess with their respective units.

Keep your life preserver WITH you at all times when at sea.

Leave it in your bunk when in Port and when you leave the ship.

DO NOT SMOKE in berthing spaces at any time or on open deck (main deck) at night.

SMOKING ALLOWED in messing spaces on deck 2 at night until "tattoo" is sounded. On main deck during daylight.

MATCHES and FLASHLIGHTS are NOT allowed in the ship. Smoking lamps are provided in messing spaces instead of matches.

Remember that an exposed light may result in discovery of ship to an enemy.

DO NOT THROW rubbish of any kind into toilet or wash troughs (this includes tobacco bags and heavy paper).

IT IS FORBIDDEN TO THROW ANYTHING OVERBOARD in the DAYTIME. Garbage will be thrown overboard at night. All wooden boxes and other articles that will float will be sent to the fire-room and burned. Metal boxes and cans will be punched with holes and thrown overboard at night. Do not place anything in garbage cans that will float.

Use your own cup for drinking water and help prevent disease.

Wash your mess-gear in TUBS provided in messing spaces.

Wash your face and hands in BAISINS provided around the sides of messing spaces.

When the General Alarm gong is sounded you will "fall in" as follows.

Men assigned to Life Boats will "fall in" abreast their respective boats.

Men in 3B, 4B, 3C and 4C will "fall in" by units in Troop mess-space, 2C.

Men in 3D and 4D will "fall in" 2D.

Men in 3G and 4G will "fall in" 2G.

Men in 3H, 4H, 3J and 4J will "fall in" 2H.

Men in 2J will stand by bunks in 2J.

In case of Abandon Ship, remember there is lots of time and every man must wait for call.

Any man starting a stampede will be shot in his tracks.

Troops may use following spaces for recreation:--

Deck C, outside Officer's quarters.

Deck I, forward and abaft of Deck-House to space roped off for Guns Crew.

Troops must habitually remain in parts of ships to which assigned.

DO NOT CROWD OR RUSH. To do so will cause confusion and possible loss of life.

Consult Bulletin Board for your station at Abandon Ship.

"Instructions for the troops" when traveling on the troop ships to Europe

World War 1 trench warfare

in. This ship was a freight vessel
and the bunks have been built in where
they put the freight Side View
End view Space in between the bunks up and down about 2 to 2½ ft.
Space in between the rows about 1 to 1½ ft.

Hand made diagram of John DeWitt's actual sleeping quarters on the General Grant

Six star general John "Black Jack" Pershing, commander of the AEF (American Expeditionary Force) in WW1

Fetid conditions of the trenches

Soldiers using their "best friend," the gas masks to protect them from chemical weapons

Trench Runners taking advantage of a chance to eat

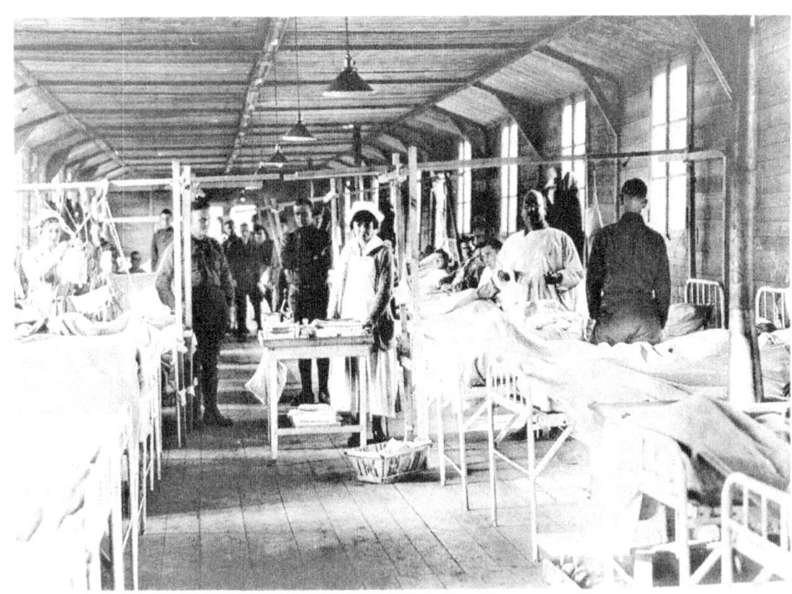

Example of a military hospital in WW1

Back row (left to right): The author, Jack Chase, Maribeth DeWitt Chase and John DeWitt. Front row (left to right): Gypsy (the Springer Spaniel), Claire Chase, Helen DeWitt and the author's sister, Kit. Circa 1971.

FIFTEEN

JOHN DEWITT'S MONTHS of training and the finely honed instincts for self-preservation he had refined since combat began near Luneville could not have prepared him for the letter he received from his mother in mid-April. 1918.

His blessed good luck in the face of many challenges had run out. His mother's news must have been as devastating as a direct hit from a German howitzer.

Helen, the woman my grandfather wrote so effusively about, the one person in his world whose absence or lack of attention seemed to make him anxious, had gone off and gotten married!

Helen had won his heart, and my normally unflappable grandfather needed to hear from her, or about her. In his letters home he never failed to mention a gift or a letter from Helen.

To make a bad situation worse, Helen had left it to a friend to tell his mother, who relayed the news to my grandfather in France. Judging from his initial reaction—adamant denial that such an event could have occurred—the news hit him hard.

His mother's letter is lost to history. I would not be surprised if my grandfather had torn it up and tossed it away. Judging from his response on April 11, I'm guessing his mother began her note with a preamble trying to soften the news.

Her letter must have been masterfully written. A mother knows, and she surely had agonized over how to tell her son the love of his life had found another. A man in combat does not need unwanted distractions, especially a broken heart.

My grandfather's response was typical:

> *You had me scared for a minute or two when I first opened your letter of the [March] 14th. I thought surely something had happened to Dad or one of the girls or my family as a whole. I am surprised that you would think that a little thing like Helen's marriage would have any serious effect on me. Of course I was some surprised for a short while.*

Blindsided by what must have been heart-breaking news, John DeWitt wrote *"a little thing like Helen's marriage."*

John Ryder DeWitt was not a man to complain or show his true feelings.

Grampa's feigned nonchalance about combat and life in the trenches—which came through repeatedly in his letters—belied his true thoughts, whatever they might have been. Everything is fine and dandy, he would write even after he'd seen friends killed in battle.

I've come to view that reaction as my grandfather's paramount defense mechanism, and I found his ability to shut things off admirable—a sign of his unimpeachable courage. That he used the same faux indifference when the love of his life walked away without even talking to him confirms my instinct.

Whatever he truly felt about Helen's marriage he kept to himself.

My response to the drama as it emerged through his letters was a little different from his. More than a hundred years later, I was upset at Helen's indifference to my Grampa's feelings. I thought, my God, she didn't even do him the courtesy of a Dear John letter, which in his case would have been ironically apt. Having a friend tell his mother about her marriage instead of writing him herself showed a callousness that annoyed me because he didn't deserve that.

I'm extremely grateful she ended it, of course, because I would not be here if they'd married. But after seeing how much he had written home about Helen, I knew she was very special to him. She could have been more understanding and tactful given the circumstances. Her sudden and heartless dumping of my dear Grampa gives literal meaning to the expression, "All is fair in love and war."

It turns out the most destructive assault my Grampa would suffer during the war was one on his heart and his plans for the future after he returned to Iowa after the war. Whatever he had in mind, he would not be doing anything with Helen.

I knew nothing about Helen until I had read his letters a hundred years later, when I became intrigued by the mysterious Helen he seemed to write so effusively about.

When I first started reading the letters, I assumed the Helen he mentioned frequently in his letter was my grandmother, Helen Brennan DeWitt, who, I'd learn later, he had met after the war. As I dug further into my family history, I would learn my Grandfather was surrounded by Helens, all of whom he mentioned in his notes home. There was Helen Fisher, apparently a good friend, his sister Helen, and Helen Irwin, who I would deduce was much more than a friend.

Helen Irwin had won his heart. When he didn't hear from her, he seemed to need to at least to hear from someone who had. Grampa was smitten with Helen Irwin.

At Camp Dodge in August 1917, he mentioned to his mother that Helen had not shown up for what I assume must have been a parade shortly before the men left for Camp Mills.

> *August 30, 1917*
>
> *Des Moines, Thursday, 3:00 PM*
>
> *Dearest Mother,*
>
> *I suppose you and Dad reached home okay, except dead tired. How does Dad feel? I suppose you know that Helen didn't come. Ought to have a letter explaining why this afternoon*

Were there cracks in the romance from the start?

My grandfather would often mention packages and gifts Helen had sent him, and after the *President Grant* returned to New York, there were four occasions in quick succession where Helen's absence bothered him when nothing else seemed to.

In one note to his mother:

> *Haven't heard from Helen I. since I wired her. Please call if they have a phone and see if you can get a hold of Grace and see what you can find out.*

And in a second:

> *There have been a million different rumors of what they are going to do with us. One of them is that we were going to go back to Des Moines and act as military police over the conscripts.*

> *It is now rumored that we will disembark this afternoon but we know nothing for sure. I will try and get the letters mailed. I may not get a chance. After you get through reading this, mail it at once to Helen in Davenport, Ohio.*

And back on board his second ship en route to Europe:

> *Write Helen and let her know that you heard from me or send her this letter if you will.*

Landing in England, about to go to war:

> *Send this letter to Helen, will you please? I will try and find time to write you both from now on.*

By then, I was reasonably certain Helen was more than a friend. He confirmed my instincts in a letter from his barracks in France.

> *I have tacked up the picture of Dad, you and myself and the one of the girls and I and one of Helen so when I am laying down, I have you all right before my eyes.*

And if I needed any more clarity, it became very clear after his Christmas reveal.

> *Well it is almost time to go to bed, that is one thing we certainly get enough of over in this country, sleep. I want to write Helen a short note tonight without fail because a year ago tonight we had some experiences and a swell time.*

"Some experiences and a swell time?

I for one did not need to know any more. Nor did I want to know what "some experiences and a swell time" meant for my pious and devoutly Catholic grandfather. Some things are best left unexplored.

But it was clear to me the boy was in love as 1918 began. And Helen was still writing him. On January 26, he'd told his mother about a gift box from Helen, mailed in December:

> *I finally got Helen's box with a wristwatch, carton of cigarettes, 2 pound box of candy and some nuts.*

On February 8, 1918, he ended a letter with a request:

> *Drop Helen F. and Irwin a short note for me please.*

That would be the last time he mentioned Helen Irwin before his mother's bombshell revelation.

When I was growing up, naturally, Helen Irwin was not a topic of conversation at family gatherings, nor was she brought up when my grandfather talked about his war experiences, which of course he never did. I can only surmise my grandfather knew her in Council Bluffs before the war and they had some friends in common.

I do know from reading through the letters that Helen Irwin was not sitting at home waiting for my grandfather to return.

In various letters he reports that Helen was in Salt Lake City and Ogden, Utah, and in Denver, apparently traveling with a female friend named Cecil. It was Cecil who informed his mother that Helen had married.

Grampa's first reaction, other than asking why his mother thought such a trifling thing as Helen Irwin's marriage would bother him, was denial.

In his April 11 response to the news, he wrote:

> *I am waiting to hear from her or Cecil to confirm it. Then I will write her a nice long letter of congratulations. I wish that if you hadn't done so already, that you write her one also. Do this please Mother.*
>
> *I had a letter from Cecil written on February 28th that she does not even intimate any such happening. Don't destroy her letters but keep them.*
>
> *What hurts most of all is that she was married in Lent. If she was married?*

It is testimony to my grandfather's devotion to his Catholic faith that he would use Lent—a time for prayer, abstinence and fasting—as a reason why his beloved could not have been married. Perhaps she was not as devout, I thought. Perhaps he did not know her that well.

I had come to learn that my grandfather was a realist despite his earnest attempts to keep things light for his mother. His doubts that Helen could have been married—perhaps moved along by the fact that she had stopped writing him—began to fade.

The doubts, justifiably, I felt, were replaced by anger.

I agreed full-heartedly with him when he wrote his mother on May 28:

> *Mighty glad to know that Cecil visited you and was sure surprised, to say the least, at what she told you of Helen's marriage. I also say she must have been drunk or crazy. I certainly feel sorry for her. I am surprised that you know that you thought I might not take a sensible view of the affair.*

Good for Grampa, I thought. Drunk or crazy made sense to me.

By June, John DeWitt had been running messages through the trenches at great peril for more than two months. I think the very real possibility of being killed served as a distraction from the battles of his love life.

By June 18 the shock of Helen's marriage had dissipated, and the news absorbed. Grampa was fine. I was not surprised. The man I knew growing up was not one to hold grudges or walk around angry at perceived insults. He was over Helen and they were writing each other again.

> *Glad to know that Helen Irwin wrote you. I had a letter from her with two snapshots of her.*

Helen and Grampa would continue to write each other, having reached their own armistice months before the one that would end the war in November.

All was forgiven. Life moved on.

Helen Irwin disappeared until we found the letters a hundred years later.

SIXTEEN

BEGINNING A JOB that is all but assured to get you killed might not be the recommended escape from the pain of being jilted, but it was all John DeWitt had.

My grandfather had no time to sit back and digest the news of Helen Irwin's marriage and the stinging rejection that came with it. Dodging incoming artillery and simply trying to survive life in the trenches can serve as a welcome distraction from matters of the heart.

By mid-April he had begun his new assignment as battalion runner, with lessons for the first time being taught in combat, under fire.

The focus of his new job, to say nothing of his own thoughts about his imminent and unpleasant demise each time he ran, seemed to have done the trick for the Helen situation. He made very little mention of his former love to his mother for the rest of the war.

To help, my Grampa had his buddies in the trenches to talk to. His friends, their companionship, and their shared misery meant much to him, as did occasional meetings with buddies from back in Council Bluffs who were in France serving with different units.

In his long April 11 letter back home, the one in which he addressed Helen Irwin's marriage, he mentions two boys from Iowa:

Ted and Phil are just fine. I saw Ted last night. He is in another village. I have had several nice long talks with him the past week. Phil just went by and said he would be back and talk to me in a little while.

It was a busy April 1918 for the 168th and the Rainbow Division, with a steady stream of raids and patrols, though the main German offensive was more to the north and west of where they had dug in, in the Baccarat section, along about thirteen miles of the front.

According to *The Story of the Rainbow Division,* with a month already in the trenches, the men "began to feel at home," though I believe that the author's implied comfort for the men in the stench of the trenches was a bit of a stretch if not an outright untruth.

John Taber painted a more realistic picture:

"A windy billet might be preferable to an air-tight dugout that dripped water onto the wretched bunks and thence to the flooded floor. It was not cheering to stand on post through the long watches of the night, rendered more miserable by the necessity of wearing shoes and clothing continuously wet, gas masks, and side arms. There were no rubber boots, no changes of shoes or socks, and the trenches were in many places knee-deep in mud and water. Long exposure to these conditions confirmed the belief that Hell is not a place of fire and brimstone, but of mud and water."

Despite the mud and water, soldiers were required also to continue to work on improving trench defenses and completing their training.

"Every man was given an opportunity to become proficient in his own fighting specialty, whether that was stringing telephone wires, digging trenches, sniping, hauling ammunition, observing artillery fire, or cooking army rations," according to Raymond Tomkins in the *History of the Rainbow Division*.

For John DeWitt, that meant refining the skills he needed to deliver messages and return to his bunk in one piece.

In that same April 11 letter, he wrote:

> *Most of the time now I am not right with the Company. I am attached to Battalion Headquarters and move with them. I am a Battalion Runner, that is, depending on Al Wallrath, my partner and a friend of Mrs. Sprague to keep the line of communication between here and Company.*
>
> *When have everything real nice and a great deal more freedom and etc., then if we were with the Company. I have no Corporal, which is very nice. Tell Dad I have all the promotions I want at present as I would rather have this job than I would of Corporal with the Company.*

My grandfather relished the job, and not once in any letter home did he complain about its rigors and his own perishability. The job came with extra comforts, apparently, that he enjoyed. The more I learned about the history of runners during the war, it seemed to me that no matter what enticements the Army used to keep its runners happy, on the grand scale of things, those comforts were hardly worth the daily chance of being blown to bits or cut down by sniper fire.

Using human runners to deliver crucial messages about troop movements, battle conditions, plans of attack, and changes of strategy proved more reliable than any other form of communication. In 1918, as my grandfather was getting his feet wet—so to speak—wireless communication was still primitive, and commanders would use colored flares, mirrors, bugles, and trained dogs to relay messages between units.

Runners were more dependable than any of those methods. A runner could memorize complicated messages and avoid the danger of having written notes fall into German hands. Runners, fit, trained, and above all, familiar with the maze of trenches, could get to hard-to-find places to deliver details that meant life or death for many.

Because they were expendable and often killed, runners were usually low-ranking non-commissioned offers, like my grandfather, a corporal. I'm certain his intellect, coolness under pressure, genial demeanor, and natural leadership had attracted the attention of his superiors. He would have fit the criteria they needed for runners. One account I read noted that runners were "chosen for their fitness, stamina and ability to read maps."

Though he smoked cigarettes like a chimney, John DeWitt had been chosen to train for the runner's job at Camp Mills. Everyone smoked, I suspect, and the habit was not something that set anyone apart as a pariah, as it is today. Runners also had to be adaptable, tough, and resourceful enough to find their destination in any sort of weather, while making their way over, around, and through various obstacles in their path.

Almost certain death aside, the job was challenging on other fronts as well. Traveling over even short distances between command posts in the mud increased the odds of being bogged down. Bogged down runners made for good targets for the always vigilant German snipers. By the time my grandfather began running in 1918, years of artillery bombardment had created a landscape of water-filled craters to avoid.

Runners carried less equipment than soldiers on the line to make them more mobile—usually a sidearm, a small knapsack, a canteen, and by the time John DeWitt was running messages, a gas mask. For any runner, the question at hand each time they ventured out was not whether they would survive, but how long before they would be wounded or killed.

My grandfather being the man he was, never mentioned his fragile odds to his mother or family. He continued to write of things with his normal light touch.

His April 18 letter home was typical.

> *Don't worry that we have any trouble spending our money. It goes before you know it. A franc, which is worth 20 cents, but it only goes as far as a nickel goes back home. We expect to get our March pay in a day or so. Eggs cost us all the way from 3 to 5 francs a dozen. Where we are now, they cost 5 francs. I ate a dozen yesterday for dinner but I have often done that and a half dozen is just a lunch. A friend of mine ate four dozen eggs during the day yesterday.*
>
> *Then we buy potatoes and fry them and made chocolate and oh we have some feeds.*
>
> *We sure have a peach of a place to stay in right now. It sure is swell. We have a nice fireplace with a good fire in it too.*

Because my grandfather would not speak of his running in any detail, and because I wanted to learn as much as I could about his experiences, I turned to John Taber's *The History of the 168th.*

I found Taber's descriptions of the runners he had served with as close to John DeWitt's experiences as I'd find.

I was intrigued at how Taber, an officer, viewed runners in the 168th. It is clear he respected them and their bravery, but it seems to me he also saw them as expendable—cogs in the system of war, commodities to be used to advance.

In one account in *The History of the 168th,* Taber wrote:

> *About five o'clock, when word was received that the fire was falling with increasing violence on the right of the sector, Company C, which was being held in readiness, was directed to take up position to the rear of P. A. Colcombet. In less than twenty minutes Captain Horton started a runner from his post of command in the quarry with the information that he was in position and in liaison with Captain Haynes.*
>
> *Half past five. An hour had passed since the beginning of the bombardment, and still no word from the front. Captain Haynes sends a runner out into the storm to get a report from the line, but the lad comes back, well-nigh exhausted, saying that it is impossible to get through. The communicating trenches are leveled, and the ground surface an impenetrable mass of debris and wire which is still writhing under the enemy barrage. Captain Haynes must know what is happening at his forward posts, and there is but one way to get the information.*
>
> *"Finch."*
>
> *"Here, Sir."*
>
> *"Go out to G. C. 9, find Lieutenant Spaulding, and bring me word of the situation.'*

"Yes, Sir", and Finch is gone. In fifteen minutes he comes stumbling down the dugout steps.

"I tried, Captain, but couldn't make it", he pants; and as he looks into the captain's eyes he sees beneath the look of human sympathy the stern necessity of things that must be done. A sudden resolution seizes him, and before the captain has turned to pick a man for the third attempt,

"I'm going back, Captain, and this time I'll get through."

Again, he is gone.

Through the inferno of bursting shells, through the tangle of brush and wire and debris, picking himself out of the mud where concussion has hurled him, stumbling over craters, Finch makes his way. Meanwhile Private Travoni is risking his life times over on a similar errand to G. C. 10 to get word from Lieutenant Fraser. He is breathless and soaked from head to foot, for the only shelter he can find when the shells break too close is in the water-filled trenches to the side. By some miracle these two reach their destinations in safety and return to P. A. 5 with the information that D Company's front is unbroken.

Our own machine gun barrage sings with threatening nearness overhead, and enemy bullets cut the surface of the road about his feet and bury themselves in the ground around him. Twice explosions knock him sprawling, but each time, bruised and shaken, he regains his footing and struggles on.

It is nearly six o'clock. The group at Battalion Headquarters nervously eye each other. So far not a single indication of what has happened on the firing line has reached

> *them. Five runners have returned to their post defeated, unable to break through the shrieking barrier of steel. Then, into the room where Colonel Tinley waits, stumbles Shephard, disheveled, blood-flecked, torn by wire, dripping with mud, exhausted.*
>
> *"Young man, I salute you", says the Battalion Commander, straightening up and raising his hand to his forehead. A faint smile plays at the lips of the runner as he falls unconscious into a pair of steadying arms.*

Such trials were part of John DeWitt's untold story.

I thought again about my grandfather's note to me in 1972, and the yellowed copy of *The Stars and Stripes* recounting Billy Schupp's death—the note I did not see until 2022, more than 100 years after his time in the trenches.

Those two items had started me on the search to discover exactly who John Ryder DeWitt was.

As far as I can tell, that note to me and his son Jack DeWitt was the first time my grandfather mentioned the stark danger of trench running and how frequently he had had put his life on the line to anyone in our family. His letters to his daughter, my mother Maribeth, years later, when she was away at college, did not go into detail about the death and destruction. Even then, years after he had returned to Iowa, started his law practice and began a family, he was protecting those close to him from the stains of the violence he'd lived through.

I felt the need to go back and look at both the note and the article again. I pulled out the folder where I had placed them. In 1972, I was 18 years old, not much younger than he was in France. I had lived an entirely different life than he had, one free of trenches and artillery bombardments and running messages between command posts under sniper fire.

In 1972, the only battles I was concerned with were on the football field, where coaches loved to use stale combat euphemisms to describe our struggles on the field. I was safe then, protected and naïve. I had not watched my friends die, nor did I ever spend a night in an abysmal and dangerous trench as artillery rained down. I was a lucky boy, carefree and safe in my environment.

We had lived different lives, my grandfather and me.

Reading the note and the article again 100 years later, I counted my blessings. I had had none of the struggles my Grampa had faced. By then, 2022, I was retired from my orthopedic surgery practice and had gained the perspective on life I lacked at 18 years old.

What was he trying to tell me when he sent me that note and the article in 1972? Why did he wait? He would die only a year later, and I wondered again if he knew that his time was running out. Had he begun to feel the symptom of the colon cancer that would kill him? Was that what, finally, after decades of interring those memories, prompted him to share them with his son and grandson?

Reading them again, eight months into my research, the note and article meant so much more to me than the first time I saw them. Then, I was shocked and surprised at what my quiet grandfather had been through, but I had only a vague sense of what it was.

The terseness of the note to me was typical of Grampa.

> *You have asked me about my war experiences.*
>
> *I told you I was a Battalion runner, but I don't think it meant a great deal to you.*

The *Stars and Stripes* article laid it out clearly and colorfully:

> *The runners are the fleet youngsters who, as the battle sways and strains, keep regiment in touch with battalion, company with platoon. To let each unit know how the others are faring, above all in such fighting as the last weeks have seen. To let the nervous guns know to what lines the surging Infantrymen have reached, this is the business of the runners. The story of much that is crushed down under such verbal impediments as liaison, reconnaissance, and communication can be told in the terms of a brave boys' legs.*

Going through them a second time, I understood the man so much better. By that point in my research John Ryder DeWitt was much more to me than the one-dimensional Grampa I had known.

He never followed up on that note from 1972, never asked me what I thought about his service in the army or his time as a trench runner, or the death of Billy Schupp, the Council Bluffs boy who just as easily could have been John Ryder DeWitt.

He let it go. I had no idea he had written that note or sent that article.

Rereading the article and the note, I was overwhelmed with sadness that he hadn't brought it up again.

I wish he had.

I would have told him how incredibly proud I was at what he had done.

SEVENTEEN

I WAS AWED by John Taber's descriptions of the daily rigors of the 168th's trench runners. His colorful accounts made things very real for me—forced me to refocus on what I had imagined my grandfather might have been doing. Anyone reading his letters quickly, as I did at first, would think he was having the time of his life.

Once I was deep into my research, I realized there was much more going on.

I had to dig.

Once I realized what my grandfather was actually doing, it became incomprehensible to me that men like him and his fellow runners would put themselves through what they did, then jump up and do it again.

After I read Taber's passage on the runners, I returned to my grandfather's letters. He had begun his runner's assignment in April, and I hoped for some grittier details about his new life, maybe a bit more action.

The closest he came to broaching the subject of combat came in his long April 11 letter, when he briefly mentioned "big high explosive shells bursting, as well as shrapnel falling."

> *Well I suppose you know without any doubt that we are back in the trenches. Oh it is a great life.*

On April 18, he returned to his upbeat ways, with only a wisp of a description of war emerging.

> *We sure have a peach of a place to stay in right now. It sure is swell. We have a nice fireplace with a good fire in it too. It wouldn't be very nice if one of those big Boesch kisses comes singing its way in however. They have missed us so far although I'll have to admit, they have come close. But I will tell you more about it when I return. Just ask me about that.*

In an undated letter written toward the end of April, when he had clearly been running messages for weeks, he reported only the perks of his new assignment.

> *Mother I am just fine and dandy with the exception of some trouble with my teeth. I hope to get them fixed tomorrow. I told you before Mother that I was with Battalion Headquarters most of the time and I carry messages from here to the Company so I see the fellows right along but I live at the Battalion Headquarters. We have a peach of a room, a big wash den and nice chairs, good feather ticks, a nice fireplace, big looking glass.*
>
> *I am getting to be quite a cook. I fix myself eggs or an omelet and yesterday I cooked some French toast and it was good too. We sure have some nice place and a good time. I think I have the best job in the Company bar none*

With my grandfather's letters spread out in front of me, safe and comfortable in Florida 100 years later, I tried to reconcile the quiet, self-effacing grandfather I knew as a boy with the young and fearless man who jumped up when beckoned and ran into hell to deliver a message—then returned to do it again. I thought about Grampa and me watching football in front of the television on fall afternoons when we visited, and about walking behind him and his ample waist as I followed him slowly up the long flight of stairs to his law office in Griswold. I thought about his God-awful snoring and wondered if he did that at Battalion headquarters. It would have been as loud as incoming artillery.

I was intrigued by John Taber's descriptions of runners from the 168th—including John Ryder DeWitt—and what they had voluntarily put themselves through. My grandfather's reticence about describing to his family what he was doing left a void. I needed to find more first-hand accounts. Taber's were certainly colorful, but I wanted other perspectives.

After my first pass through the letters, I realized I would not get much from them about his fighting—which to me was the Holy Grail of this experiment, the entire point of digging into his life during the war and what he had done.

He rarely mentioned combat, inclined as always to keep his letters pleasant, almost wistfully nostalgic. As I read them, I thought his accounts sounded more like a he was at a company picnic than fighting a war. I knew he was pulling his punches. After my first pass through the batch of letters, I was disappointed, thinking there was no way I'd write a book from what I had and what he was offering. I knew also by the time I was months into my research, that it was important to read between the lines.

I needed more information, and it would not be coming from John Ryder DeWitt.

Then I remembered something I'd read when I first pored over the letters in my sister Abby's living room in Lincoln, Nebraska. That afternoon, we'd sorted the letters she'd found in our uncle's garage and put them in chronological order. Essentially, I had only skimmed them that afternoon.

I recalled one later letter in which he had encouraged his parents to read *The Saturday Evening Post* if they wanted to know what he had been doing. I vaguely remembered he had mentioned the name of a journalist.

Six months later, back in Florida and well into my research, I looked for that letter again and found it.

In an August 1918 letter my grandfather had written, with an astounding amount of candor for him, given his reluctance to discuss anything about combat and his daily routine:

> *Some of the truest and most realistic articles on the war, expressing just what a fellow feels are written by George Pattullo, who writes for the Saturday Evening Post. Read them as you would a letter from me.*

That quick jotting was precisely what I had been looking for. I had found a proxy for John Ryder DeWitt, and a voice that could fill in for his silence.

I decided I would find articles from George Pattullo in the *Saturday Evening Post* dating back to April 1918, when my grandfather had started his battalion-runner assignment. George Pattullo would help me fill in the blanks. I could learn about the things my grandfather simply left unsaid.

I found the rich archive of the magazine online and subscribed. George Pattullo was a Canadian reporter and later novelist and editor of *The Boston Herald*. Pattullo was the first to report on the heroics of World War I icon, the Tennessee sharpshooter and Medal of Honor winner, Alvin York.

I learned quickly that Pattullo was a masterful writer. Much like an embedded reporter of later wars, he travelled with the troops and spent time on the front. There was no such thing as secondary reporting for him.

I found an article from *The Post* of April 27, 1918, shortly after my grandfather had begun his running. I found it particularly apt. With the headline "Sitting on the World," Pattullo writes of a typical night in the trenches with an unidentified group of American soldiers, providing a spare but evocative account of life under fire:

> *The hour was midnight, the dugout had a door but it was wide open, and the portiere of sacking which kept in the light failed entirely to keep out the cold.*
>
> *"Call me a runner, will you?"*
>
> *"Coming," replied a voice.*
>
> *The night was clear and frosty. A few stars glittered in the sky, but it was plenty black enough for dirty work.*
>
> *The runner came stumbling along the duckboards and we descended into the dugout. I noted with satisfactions there appeared to be ten to twelve feet of earth and stone above its stout roof. Every little bit helps.*
>
> *"Take this to the battalion P.C. ," ordered the company commander, "and bring me back an answer."*
>
> *"Yes, sir."*
>
> *He lifted the flap and was gone. The captain gave a tired yawn. We hard marched twelve miles to make the relief; before that officers had marched up to H. 3 to make a reconnaissance, then back., thirty-six miles in as many hours and only four hours of sleep. It takes men of fine stamina to withstand the strain of a company officer's work.*

A few minutes and steps were heard on the stairs. The flap was raised and in came a tall gangling youth in a leather jacket, carrying a rifle. He gave the captain a sort of salute and presented a note. Then he leaned his weight nonchalantly on one leg and his rifle and waited. He may have been 20 years old but looked younger, and of all the cool customers it had been my good fortune to meet, that boy carried off the palm.

"What the Sam Hill does he want now?" exclaimed the captain, opening the paper. "I bet _____"

A loud explosion interrupted him; then another and another and another. Somebody was shooting rifle grenades; somebody else was abetting him with a shower of hand grenades. A minute, and a crackling rifle fire added to the din.

"Who's doing the shooting?" the captain cried. "I told those men not to open up until the actually saw a German making for them."

"Oh, those guys over on the right've got some kind of war on," replied the runner carelessly, with the tolerance of a veteran of a dozen campaigns.

Pretty soon the noise stopped and quiet settled again over the trenches. The captain wrote a reply to the note, and the battalion runner departed.

"That's a good kid," remarked the commander. "When we were in the line for training last November he carried a message half a mile through a hell of a barrage. Never so much batted an eye, either."

My picture of my grandfather and what he had done was becoming clearer. I saw a lot of John Ryder DeWitt in the young, insouciant runner. I could imagine that would be how he'd deal with the pressure, and the officers.

If he was not going to write about what he was going through, I'd let John Taber and George Pattullo do it for him.

EIGHTEEN

I REALIZED SOMETHING else as I uncovered more details about the daily lives of soldiers in the trenches. Once I did, I forgave my grandfather his reticence. It seemed to me that writing about more peaceful events on the front reminded him of what he was fighting for—and that the world had not, in fact, gone mad.

No longer puzzled about his well-intentioned mission to keep his family away from what was going on in France, I decided to stop questioning his motives and trying to somehow dissect his motivations.

It didn't matter in the end.

His motives were simple, I knew. His mother, sisters, and father did not need to worry about him when he genuinely did not seem worried about himself. He would not interrupt their lives back in Council Bluffs. His mother had plenty of concerns herself, not the least of which was a husband in ill health and the accompanying concerns that arise when the breadwinner can't work.

My grandfather had the gift of empathy. He genuinely cared for his family. Empathy for others was a trait he continued to carry for the rest of his life.

I decided, finally, to stop worrying about his cheeriness, feigned or not. I knew I could learn what he'd gone through by other means.

An early April letter triggered my decision to let it go. He continued to be a chipper as ever, even while the 168th was involved in heavy fighting.

> *After several days of cloudy weather, today is certainly a splendid one. The sun is shining and everything is just fine. I am in the best of health and feeling fine.*

April was a month of heavy combat for the 168th. Heavy combat meant streams of messages to deliver for John DeWitt and his cohorts. Each time a unit was engaged, important communications would be written down, memorized by the runners, delivered, and responded to. When he was at the front, I doubt my grandfather sat still through much of April and May. The raids were relentless.

As April softened the March chills, the men of the 168th became inured to the combat that for them had now become de rigueur. There was no getting around the fact that nearly every night groups of men went out to either find enemy posts or set up ambushes to capture German prisoners. At least they had warmer weather to do so.

With the Americans becoming more aggressive the Germans turned more cautious and, according to *The Story of the Rainbow Division* by Raymond S. Tompkins, published in 1919, "gradually relinquished to us the almost unchallenged control of No Man's Land."

> *The temper of the regiment was manifested not only by the organized parties which made their nightly pilgrimages into German territory, but by the willingness of the men to go out at any time during the day or the night after any of the enemy who had the temerity to show themselves.*

On April 4 a patrol investigating what appeared to be a suspicious German nest, found it deserted but returned with a box of high explosives and a large coil of wire.

On April 19 a patrol of some 70 men made its way to a string of old shell holes near the German line, marked by barbed wire, looking for an opening under heavy fire. Foiled at first, they were undeterred, waited until the time was right, and successfully breeched the opening and forced the Germans to run.

According to John Taber's *History of the 168th*, "this was ticklish business, penetrating into the enemy line when he was aware of the presence of the patrol and when he might be planning some ruse to fall upon it; but while they may have been somewhat nervous, they were stout-hearted men and it never occurred to them to hesitate."

Realizing they had found a main point of entry for the German trenches, the Iowa men set up an ambush. One of the men, hearing a cough, realized the trench was occupied. The Iowans tossed in grenade and withdrew to the safety of their own lines. "The night's work was done, and they could return to their billets in Badonviller to sleep and to prepare for the next night's adventure."

The raids did not always go well. On April 21, a cold, dark, and rainy night, a party of three officers and five men approached the German wire and took cover in a shell hole. Passing through the wire into German territory, an American coughed. The Germans sent up a flare in response as the Americans took cover.

"With their hearts in their mouths, and the mere tick of their watches sounding to their ears like hammers on an anvil, they resumed their wary course," Taber wrote.

The Germans found the American patrol quickly and attacked, capturing and killing an officer, leaving his body for the Americans to find.

By the beginning of May, according to the *History of the Rainbow Division,* the now-seasoned soldiers had reached a point where they "could be pushed just so fur and no fu'ther."

John Taber would write that, back in the trenches after these nightly raids, the men had only three things to look forward to. I know my grandfather would have been a happy young man as he waited for any of them: "Chow, relief, and the occasions when Chaplain Robb, loaded up like a Santa Claus with tobacco, cigarettes, and candy (if he could unearth any), came to distribute good cheer."

They were men at war and Chaplain Robb was responsible for their fragile morale—"entrusted with the spiritual welfare of the men, and burying the dead, and keeping a record of the burials, he acted as banker, general purchasing agent, and athletic director of the regiment."

The chaplain was also the editor of a newspaper, *The Wild Rose,* which had begun back at Camp Mills and continued in France to bring news from the outside world, and to entertain, as much as it could, with cartoons and opinion columns and, on occasion, poetry.

"While it lasted," Taber wrote, "*The Wild Rose* was a distinct influence in the life of the regiment."

Given my grandfather's loquaciousness, I was surprised that he apparently did not write for *The Wild Rose*. I supposed he contented himself with his almost daily letters home.

Signs that April that the tide of the war was turning in favor of the Allies were evident from an article in the April 26, 1918, *Stars and Stripes,* covered by a front-page headline:

BATTLE'S NEW PHASE
INDECISIVE AS FIRST
German Attacks Gain some Ground
But No Objective Is Won—
Drain on Enemy Manpower Exceeds Verdun

When on Sunday of this week, the first month of the German offensive came to an end, the enemy had thrown into the fight at total of 130 Divisions, or nearly 2,000,000 men. In his desperate lunges forward he had been obliged to use as many troops in four weeks as he had used in Verdun in four months.

In miles he is little nearer Paris and the Channel ports than he was before, but despite the heavy price he has paid and for all the violence of his effort, he has gained no measurable strategic advantage. In reality, he is not near those objectives. He is no nearer in the sense that there is today no more reason for thinking he can attain them than there was before he offensive was launched.

The men of the 168th must have taken heart that they were making progress—that the American effort was producing positive results and the Germans were back on their heels.

John DeWitt was certainly gratified and, as always, nostalgic and proud of his service.

In his very busy April 11 letter, the one in which he very quickly mentioned he was now a battalion runner, he wrote of the people at his peacetime job at the Messco company.

Well Mother, I had two nice long letters from Messco one from Carl, my old boss and one from Rosie the Steno.

In the mix with his letters home, my sister and I found another letter, typed and addressed to W. R. Butler, "alias Bill," presumably the head of the Messco company my grandfather was clearly fond of. His letter to Butler shows his pride in what he was doing in France and the reason he was there.

The letter is quite effusive but even then, my grandfather refrains from going into any level of detail that would capture what he and the others were going though.

Despite his enthusiasm for the "old Mesco style" by the time John DeWitt had returned to Iowa he had set his sights on a more ambitious undertaking, law school. Still, his life before the war seemed to be a satisfying one.

April 25, 1918
[Typed letter to Mr. W.R. Butler (alias Bill)]

Dear Sir:

Just a few lines from an old Messco booster who is "over here" doing his bit in the old Messco style, doing his damnedest to "halt the hun".

It is a great ole' existence "over here" but I am enjoying the greater part of it, enjoying the best of health, feeling fine all the time, almost anyway and plenty of old pep on hand for all occasions. We have a great many inconveniences "over here" and have to endure hardships at times but taking it as a whole, I don't believe we have it as hard as the average individual believes. That is, except when we are fighting up here in the line but at that I wouldn't be back there [in Council Bluffs] unless this business is finally settled for a considerable sum.

Of course you won't remember me but I was a member of the good ole' department 16 and 17 under that genial gentleman, Mr. J.C. Gelwick. Often my thoughts strayed back to the many happy hours spent there. The night work was pleasant.

Judging from the newspapers we have received from home, they are keeping you extremely well informed as to our progress in a military way.

Us boys who are "over here" facing the music will consider it an easy and pleasant task on our return to sell a merchant already heavily stocked with competitors merchandise.

The military terms found sprinkled throughout the weekly newsletter and especially while mentioning the imaginary battle between the Companies A and B are amusing. I will venture the fellows little realize what a depth of meaning they have in actual combat.

The individual who was instrumental in having weekly newsletters sent to the former Messco boys now in the service little realizes what good he has done the firm. I enjoy reading them as much as any letter. While busy reading them, the house and its associates are vividly pictured in my mind as I know them. They will do a great deal towards cementing what might be called a profitable friendship for the house.

Strange though it may seem, I find myself comparing incidents of this life to those of my days spent with the house.

I received the Thanksgiving and the Christmas letters which the house sent out and also a Christmas box from the house, also a Christmas box from the Messco boys and girls. On the receipt of each and every one of them, I experienced that sensation generally described as a warm feeling around the heart. Such things as these mean an awful lot to us fellows "over here". Let the good work go on.

I started out to write a few lines but was carried away by the theme and find it reaching the limits as set by the censor.

Haven't received any "buzz saw" for quite a while, hoping it is not a thing of the past. I wish you would convey my best regards to the members of the firm and I wish to thank them for what they have done for us and such things help mightily.

Hoping this finds you and everyone connected with the firm enjoying the best of health and the best of spirits.

Yours very sincerely,
John R. DeWitt

I uncovered more about my grandfather's family dynamic in his April letters. One impediment to learning as much as I could about John DeWitt's life through those letters was the fact I was essentially eavesdropping on a one-way conversation. His mother's letters were long gone. I learned to read between the lines and to imagine what she had written him.

It seems my Grampa and his mother shared the same trait of eternal optimism, or at least they both refrained from including any bad news in their respective missives.

In April and May of 1918, I gathered from my grandfather's letters to his mother that his father was not in the best of health—though apparently his mother did not go into detail. His father would die in 1920 at age 58, so the senior DeWitt never recovered from whatever was ailing him. I gathered also that the family's finances were strained, because the elder DeWitt continued to work his railroad job into his mid-50s at a time when the average life expectancy for an American male was 54.

My grandfather worried about his father's health. In a May 6, 1918, letter to his mother he expressed his concern.

> *Monday, May 6, 1918*
>
> *Bad news in the fact that dear ole' Dad o' mine was sick again. Sure sorry to hear that and only wish I was able to be there and help.*
>
> *Tell Dad to stick with it if possible and then when I get back, we will see if he can't quit the railroad game. It must mean a lot of hard work for you Mother but your letters would never let one know, they are always so cheerful and encouraging for one to do his best.*

Following up the next day, my pious grandfather swore—God forbid—if only slightly—a brazen and profane act for the good son.

> *Tuesday, May 7, 1918*
> *At the Front*
>
> *Your dear letter of April 8th was received last night. Glad you and Ann went to the dance and had a good time. Sure is too bad about Dad. Tell him he had best take better care of himself or he will catch (may I say it just this once Mother) hell from me when I get back. Conditions at home are the only thing that make me regret being over here. Do the best you can until I can get there to help things along.*

I can only imagine, given his closeness to his father, that his father's health weighed heavily on his mind, as if he needed more to be concerned about. Such things can be a serious distraction and impediment to a soldier's health and welfare in combat.

The powers that be were aware of the need to keep morale high, and the effort to do so was a major concern for the leaders of the American Expeditionary Force, who recognized that men could not fight in an uninterrupted stream of daily combat. They needed relief, and in an early April note home, my grandfather noted the importance of time off, away from the front.

> *I must say now that I can't say too much about the wonderful work that the YMCA is doing for us boys over here. Up to the present, I have seen nothing of the KC or Knights of Columbus or Salvation Army organizations on this part of the line. The YMCA is with us wherever we go and first things the fellows want to know when they land in a new place is where is the Y?*

In a May 6 letter, he once again noted its importance.

> *A couple nights ago two good looking American girls put on a splendid entertainment at the Y. They were mighty good and it sure did one worlds of good just to look at them. They also appeared here again last night but I didn't go and I wish I had now.*

To prevent soldiers from breaking down emotionally and physically, soldiers would spend four to six days in the front trenches, in combat, before moving back to secondary—and thus safer—trenches, then move farther back to the reserve trenches, where they could relax before starting the process again.

Free time in reserve areas meant a chance to spend time at a YMCA hut and in general to simply relax as much as possible. Seeing it as a way to keep up morale, fitness, and soldiers out of trouble, the Army encouraged the men to get involved in sports while relaxing at the rear, baseball being the most popular.

Grampa, I knew, was not much of a jock. His only interest in later years in Iowa was golf. Perhaps he felt, no doubt warranted, that his time running messages through heavy fire qualified him for a lifetime exemption from strenuous exercise when he got back home.

According to a 1919 book, *The Americans in the Great War, by* Richard Joseph Beamish and Francis Andrew March, "Nothing gave greater relaxation to the fighting man, coming from the trenches, or the battle line caked with mud and blood and weary with long hours, than a shower bath, and generous facilities were provided close to the fighting front."

> *The club life of the army and navy, both in the training camps and after the men went into the service, was most capably directed by the Y. M. C. A., Knights of Columbus, and the Jewish Welfare Association. Non-sectarianism was the rule in all of the huts and clubs conducted by these organizations. Catholic, Protestant and Jewish chaplains mingled with workers of the Salvation Army, with professional prize-fighters who became athletic instructors, with actors and actresses who contributed their talents freely to the entertainment of soldiers and sailors. Moving-picture shows, boxing contests, continuation schools, canteens where women workers*

> *served American-made dishes—these were some of the activities following the men. The YMCA and Knights of Columbus bore the largest share of this work. More than $300,000,000 was contributed by the people of America to the maintenance of these activities.*

Being behind the lines and being in a YMCA did not mean one was safe from the war. Marion Crandall, a Cedar Rapids native, who had graduated from the Sorbonne in Paris, returned to France in January 1918 after teaching French at St. Katherine's School in Davenport.

She felt her fluent French and knowledge of the country could help American soldiers.

Marion Crandall became the first American woman to die in a combat zone when the YMCA canteen where she was working was hit by German artillery shells on March 27, 1918.

For John DeWitt, the war would become very real.

NINETEEN

MAY 1918 WAS unlike anything John DeWitt and the rest of the Iowa 168th had experienced—four turbulent weeks of continuous raids into No Man's Land bookended by two memorable events.

The month began with an unrelenting American bombardment of the German lines that started in the early morning hours of May 1. It ended with an ominous and lethal phosgene gas attack on the Americans that killed or maimed scores of men on May 27.

Still, despite the clamor, things were beginning to look up. The Americans were starting to make a difference in the four-year-old war, though the advances came at a great price.

Patrols left the safety of the American lines to the point where they seemed nonstop. The Americans began to feel they dominated No Man's Land. If he did not already know by then, weeks into his job as a battalion runner, John Ryder Dewitt had learned that war was a serious and unforgiving enterprise.

The phosgene attack at the end of the month, besides offering a taste of the depths to which both the Germans and Allies had sunk, prompted my grandfather to mention the possibility of his own demise to his mother, which of course he shrugged off. In his letter home, he only hinted at the gas attack that caused his introspection—dancing, I suppose, with the censors about how much he could reveal.

The attack had left him uncharacteristically pensive.

> *May 28, 1918*
> *At the Front*
>
> *Well Mother dear, this is about all the news here I am able to tell. I think the people of Iowa will get quite a shock between now and when you get this letter.*
>
> *Don't ever worry about me when you hear rumors, which I suppose circulate around. Wait until you get official notification from Washington. If I am called, you may rest assured I am not afraid to go to the Maker and that I am better off.*
>
> *There is no reason to be alarmed. I just thought this was as good a time as any to write it.*
>
> *That gas is certainly awful stuff. I fear that more than anything else.*

May was a month of heated battles, and for battalion runners, an abundance of chances to tease fate, or as my grandfather phrased it, opportunities to meet his Maker. The momentum for the war had turned in favor of the Americans and Allies and he was swept up in the current.

The May 1 assault on the German line was an impressive display of American power and resources as the 168th dug in for the start of its fourth month of combat. Germany's spring offensive, begun on March 31 in the hope of winning the now four-year-old war before the Americans could fully insert themselves, was proving impotent.

Daily victories for the 168th, small but significant, were adding up.

May was significant for another reason. Americans began to operate independently that month after the first U.S. victory at Cantigny, just as Black Jack Pershing had planned.

By the time my grandfather arrived in Europe with the rest of the 168th four months earlier, France and Britain had already lost a combined five million men since the war began in 1914—more than twice the population of Iowa in 1918. It was a number I found incomprehensible. The Americans' arrival would change the course of the war.

The German's spring offensive was neither desperate not frantic. The Germans at the time seemed to have had the upper hand. On paper the offensive made sense. The Germans sent 3.5 million troops with superior artillery up against 2.5 million demoralized British and French troops. The Americans were in the wings, though, and ready to go, and the Germans underestimated the effect of the new American troops would have.

The war's end, still seven months off, was coming into focus as the German offensive fizzled, though horrendous battles were in store that summer for the Rainbow Division, the men of the 168th, and John Ryder DeWitt.

Looming in July was more heavy fighting at Champagne-Marne, in September at Saint Mihiel, and finally, the Argonne, part of what the leaders of the allied forces were calling the Hundred Days Offensive that ended the war.

The Americans would save the day.

My grandfather's effort to help turn the tide must have buoyed him.

In a May 6 letter home, her wrote his mother:

> *As I told you before, I am what they call a Battalion runner. Our work is responsible and we have to be on the*

> *job almost all the time. When we are in the front line, then is our busy time, all hours of the day or night.*
>
> *Now remember, I don't want you to tell this about because it is just for your information alone. I am using, for the first time, what they call a BLUE ENVELOPE. It is censored by the base censor and not by the Company officers. I am also sending you two more of The Stars and Stripes under a separate cover.*

I wondered if he sent home the Friday, May 17, 1918, edition of *The Stars and Stripes.*

That day's issue showed how much things had changed since John DeWitt had arrived in Europe. The French, skeptical at first in late 1917 as their combat-hardened veterans began training the greenhorn Americans, changed their minds after the fighting began. American troops were operating independently and successfully. They had won over the French, who at the outset of America's entry into the war the year before were hopeful but cynical.

It had been no small task.

A year and a week after the United States had entered the war *The Stars and Stripes* ran in large print across the top of its front page a quote from French premiere Georges Benjamin Clemenceau:

> *Last September, I said to several of your magnificent soldiers whose guest I was: "You are going to be called upon to make a great effort and fulfill it, perhaps at the cost of your life. We can feel only gratitude and friendship for you who have come from afar to help us."*
>
> *Today we have seen them at their task. Men who served with impassioned zeal the democratic ideal we want to save; they are worth of the great forbears. Honor to their valor.*

Honor and valor indeed.

As I learned more about the intensity of fighting in May, I came to realize that the words were more than a politician's hyperbole. For the men of the 168th and John DeWitt, honor and valor were touchstones, gauges to which they applied their actions.

John Taber wrote about the bravery that was commonplace among his men in May 1918:

> *The temper of the regiment was manifested not only by the organized parties which made their nightly pilgrimages into German territory, but by the willingness of the men to go out at any time during the day or the night after any of the enemy who had the temerity to show themselves. If a Boche sniper became too active, someone in the line would soon be around seeking permission of the officer in charge to organize a little party to get him. Or when things were getting too slack, another would think up some plan and lay it before the lieutenant. Generally, these ideas were too wild to be feasible, but they showed the proper spirit.*

THE ARRIVAL of May coincided with "the full bloom of luxuriant summer," John Taber noted, with "nature doing her best to overcome the handicaps of war."

The sweetness of the weather no doubt helped the men of the 168th deal with its accelerated role in the war. On two ranges built near Neufmaisons, men were given further instruction on the implements they would use with greater frequency in the coming weeks—handling and throwing grenades, further practice firing rifles, machine guns—and in an indication of the close-quarter fighting of the trenches, pistols and bayonets.

Another drill would prove crucial when the month ended, donning gas masks and learning how to adjust them quickly.

"The first of May was ushered in with a bang," John Taber wrote in *The History of the 168th*.

He meant it literally.

At two o'clock that morning American heavy artillery began what would be a continuous forty-eight-hour bombardment of German lines near the Grand Bois outside Badonviller—the purpose of which was to soften the line for a planned attack.

"Shells were whistling over us like a winter's wind," Taber wrote.

Taber estimated "20,000 rounds fell on the Boche opposite the Rainbow in the 1st, and on the 2nd, 33,000."

My grandfather would write home in early May complaining of ear trouble, but not pinpoint its source. I wondered if the blasting guns might have had a hand in his problems, or at the least, made them worse.

On May 6 he wrote:

> *I am feeling fine again and everything is just fine except that my ear is giving me a little trouble yet.*

Two days later, writing again, he noted that was fine,

> *I have recovered my hearing again and am mighty relieved. I couldn't hear out of my right ear and it also affected my left.*

The American attack on the German positions after the bombardment would set the tone for the month. The

Germans had built in the Grand Bois —what was described in numerous accounts as a beautiful forest—a network of wire, concrete trenches, and blockhouses they considered impenetrable. In this forest command post they had installed and concealed machine gun nests and their mobile 77-millimeter guns.

After the American and French artillery had sufficiently softened both the network and the German's resolve, a series of daring and successful raids by Rainbow Division units from Ohio and Alabama gave the Americans a solid foothold as they continued west.

With the vacuum created by my grandfather's lack of desire to describe his combat experiences, I wanted to know more about what the men were feeling now that they were being frequently cast into the fire.

I wanted confirmation of American courage, of the young men who a year earlier were untrained civilians.

I looked again to George Pattullo, the *Saturday Evening Post* reporter. Pattullo was not a kid, nor was he a rosy-cheeked optimist. He was nearly 40 when he traveled with the troops and he was not a reporter given to hyperbole or, for that matter, flag-waving. He was a straight-shooting writer with a practiced eye, the very traits that drew my grandfather and no doubt thousands of other troops to his writing.

George Pattullo understood on a very basic level the frustrations and tensions of the war, and he had a gift for conveying them to readers back home.

Pattullo knew.

And my grandfather knew that Pattullo knew.

I found an article in which he reported on a mission he accompanied in the May 27, 1918 issue of the magazine, titled "On Night Patrol."

An official report of the incident would probably phrase it, "On receipt of the order Lieutenant Cabot Lee Higginson Jones employed violent language," but that would entirely disguise his identity from his comrades and would, moreover, be doing "Bud" a grave injustice. To say he employed "violent language" is a slur; he swore like a mule skinner and I intend to give him full credit. The facts are that Lieutenant Bud Jones tossed the note from the regimental intelligence officer onto the dugout table and groaned, clawing impotently at his hair, as one in the anguish of despair.

"What do you know about the armchair bonehead?" he raved. "He sits back there and dopes out stunts on paper that nobdy'd dream of who knew anything about the lay of things."

Lieutenant Jones was only twenty-three years old and had been peacefully engaged in selling bonds for a New York City firm until the war broke, and now he was out in No Man's Land with seventeen husky doughboys, in momentary expectations of being blown to atoms by the German artillery or less messily removed from terrestrial activities by a sniper.

It was seven forty-five and biting cold. The members of the patrol, gathered in the trench, shivered as the waited. Perhaps it was because they were without overcoats—or perhaps, well, men always shiver before the go over the top over venture out into No Man's Land. Most of them coughed, though they tried to check it; a few gulped from time to time.

I chuckled over the lieutenant's "mule skinner" mouth and thought of my Grampa's apology for writing "hell" to his mother. I somehow knew John DeWitt was neither an inventive nor creative curser. I knew he did not likely get too colorful, if he swore at all. But I knew also the usual swearing among veterans in the middle of combat would not have bothered him. He was in the army after all, not a seminary, and had been for close to a year.

I wondered also if Grampa shared Lieutenant Jones's frustrations over the impenetrability of the bureaucracy that was a universal complaint of the common soldier in every war.

I wondered about my grandfather's own tensions as his climbed from a trench into heavy fire to deliver a message. I tried to picture him minutes away from stepping into the cacophony and shellfire and wondered if he took deep breaths or gulped to calm himself. I imagine he did, but I also knew those calming breaths were accompanied by silent Hail Marys.

I thought, too, of how young my grandfather had been in 1918, and how young most men who go to war usually are. And then I thought of the dead, the young men who did not live out their lives fully as my grandfather would after a long and successful life.

I was chilled by Patullo's masterful euphemism for death—of being "terrestrially removed."

With patrols seemingly heading out continuously as May progressed, both sides engaged earnestly in trying to capture prisoners. Prisoners were the best source of information about what the enemy was planning.

A prisoner taken by the Americans on May 26 warned that the Germans were planning a gas attack on the American position. It would come one day later.

The prisoner was so certain and insistent about the upcoming attack, officers interrogating him sent out a special warning to every post in the regiment.

My grandfather certainly had heard the warning, which proved all too accurate. He would have known that unless he pulled on his mask immediately, he would be burned and suffocated. He would have known he'd be lucky if he died quickly because many men would suffer for days or weeks before expiring.

It was no wonder my grandfather wrote of the possibility of his death and of his fear of gas. In addition to the physically crippling effects of gas, the psychological effects of merely thinking about being caught in a gas attack was devastating to soldiers on both sides.

Every soldier knew about gas. They had all watched comrades wither and die after inhaling the potent toxins. Close to 85 percent of the 91,000 gas deaths in World War I were from phosgene.

There was no higher moral ground. Both sides, the Germans on one hand, and the British, English and Americans on the other, used gas. Future American President Harry S Truman, a captain, commanded an artillery unit that fired poison gas at the Germans in 1918.

Early on the morning of May 27 the Germans launched gas an artillery attack on the on the American lines in the vicinity of Ville Negre. The men of the 168th were particularly vulnerable. Their lines were inundated with some 1,000 canisters while many men were asleep. There was no time to sound an alarm.

John Taber described that attack.

> *At 12:55 on the morning of the 27th a terrific crash, which might have been the explosion of a gigantic mine, rocked the entire sector from the front line back to Pexonne. Buildings shook as if in the clutch of a mighty earthquake, and the sky glowed red with a sudden flash. Those behind the lines knew that something terrible had happened, while those in it, dazed by the unexpectedness of the shock, hardly knew what to expect. A few seconds later hundreds of bulky missiles, wobbling through the air with a sickening rush, exploded in their midst, and terrified shouts of "Gas!" warned them that they were in for that greatest of horrors, a night gas attack. Gas is the one weapon that is more effective by night than by day, for darkness only heightens its effect, and the terror, confusion, and bewilderment is increased a hundredfold. In a moment half the battalion area was suddenly drenched with the concentrated fumes of phosgene gas, one whiff of which is enough to kill.*

In a particularly insidious move, the Germans fired explosive shells behind the Iowans to stop them from evacuating. As dawn broke, the firing abated and the men of the 168th were able to emerge and care for their wounded. By the end of the day, 35 men were dead and another 270 wounded.

Heroics seemed common rather than the exception.

One lieutenant, a man John Taber identified as only "Lieutenant Priddy," caught in the wave of gas, remained on duty to care for the men in his platoon instead of seeking help for himself. He died two days later and was posthumously awarded the Distinguished Service Cross.

Lieutenant Clarence Green made his way through the dark trenches with his gas mask on, warning others to be prepared. Finding the mask was making it too difficult to see and slowing him down, his simply removed it periodically to get his bearing and continue to warn as many men as he could. The gas he breathed during those short breaks would kill him the next day.

Sergeant Gordon E. Perry, gassed himself, helped carry a steady stream of incapacitated men to an aid station though he never took aid himself. The effort proved too much, and he collapsed and died.

And so it went all night and the next day.

My grandfather's luck had reinserted itself, he had been sick, he wrote his mother, and had had time to get his mask on. Writing the day after the attack, he hinted at the news of the gas attack his mother had surely heard about before his letter would arrive back in Council Bluffs.

> *I suppose you have anxiously been looking for this letter for several days.*
>
> *I have been under the weather the last few days and have not been able to write. I am feeling better today and think I will be all okay by tomorrow. I had a touch of trench fever which is quite prevalent.*
>
> *There has been a lot doing here abouts lately but the papers will undoubtedly have told you about it by the time you get this.*

He followed up five days later to reiterate he was safe and had not suffered any of the effects of the gas attack.

Sunday evening
June 2, 1918
At the Front

Dearest Mother o' mine,

I am not just sure when I wrote you last or what I told you so if I repeat, don't be surprised. I am in the best of health, feeling fine, only a little lazy.

I suppose by the time you receive this, you mothers will have done a lot of worrying. It sure is too bad that such is war. I only wish there was some way we could stop your worrying. That gas is awful stuff and it is feared but good old gas masks saved the day.

The summer of 1918 lay ahead, and with it even more combat than the extraordinary month of May had offered.

And there was yet another challenge raising its head.

Two months before, at Fort Riley, Kansas, a private named Albert Gitchell checked himself into the base hospital complaining of a sore throat, fever, and headache. Soon after one hundred more Fort Riley soldiers had done the same.

By summer, soldiers who had trained at Kansas bases like Camp Funston, Fort Riley and Camp Dodge would be arriving in Europe to fight.

With them would come a then-misunderstood condition known as the Spanish influenza.

TWENTY

MY GRANDFATHER'S GAS mask and quick reactions saved him from the German phosgene assault, but he'd very soon be laid low by a nearly invisible crawling enemy that was thriving in the filth of the trenches.

As May turned to June, the war teetered precariously on a tipping point that would soon favor the Americans.

For John DeWitt, keeping healthy and getting back home to Iowa and his family took on new meaning beyond avoiding snipers and exploding German artillery.

As the reeling 168th buried its dead and cared for the wounded, assessed the damage, and regrouped from the phosgene gas attack, some 250 miles away, German forces were approaching the outskirts of Château-Thierry, a small town 40 miles east of Paris, their Spring Offensive still churning though losing steam. Their advance was the closest the Germans had come to the French capital since 1914. The sudden attack left the Allies—without American help—surprised and unprepared.

The Germans would capture 50,000 Allied soldiers, but the attack, thanks to an enthusiastic infusion of fresh and unintimidated Americans, would be repulsed.

By June 4, the German advance was checked by stiff American resistance that prevented them crossing the Marne River. West of Château-Thierry, the 2nd Division of the American

Expeditionary Force, which included a brigade of Marines, defended the road to Paris ferociously.

The Americans' tenaciousness was precisely what the Germans had feared, and the counterattack in what became known as the Battle of Belleau Wood began to change the course of the war. By month's end the Germans knew their hoped-for goal of ending the war victoriously before the Americans could make a difference had disappeared.

The Americans would change the course of the war outside Château-Thierry, and Belleau Wood would become an iconic and hallowed battle in the years to come. The courage of the U.S. Army and Marines was such that the French renamed Belleau Wood "Bois de la Brigade de Marine"—Wood of the Marine Brigade.

Early in the brutal engagement, as the Germans pressed forward, French troops began to retreat and suggested the Americans follow suit. One Marine, Captain Lloyd W. Williams, assured himself an honored page in Marine Corps lore when he responded "Retreat? Hell, we just got here!"

I could not help but think when I read that quote, that John Ryder DeWitt felt the same way.

The victory at Belleau Wood was costly, with 1,811 Americans killed and close to 8,000 wounded before the fresh troops thwarted six separate German assaults in the difficult terrain.

Near Ville Negre, my Grandfather and the 168th girded themselves as they recovered from the gas attack. The vapor from the onslaught was so heavy as it drifted, the men who escaped injury were forced to wear masks for hours after.

Later, the Americans discovered a disquieting fact about the size of the barrage that hit them. According to John Taber:

Their shells were eighteen centimeters in diameter, each containing about two gallons of liquid phosgene. They were fired from high angled tubes, similar to trench mortars, connected in batteries of one hundred and discharged simultaneously by electricity. The projectiles contained just enough explosive to burst them on impact, thus liberating the liquid which immediately vaporized into heavy gas.

The gas and its carnage would have been enough to unsettle most soldiers. But another insidious threat had inserted itself.

The soldiers' stunned recovery effort was made much more difficult by an epidemic of trench fever, a condition so appalling that the sudden dizziness and headaches that came with it could lead to soldiers abruptly keeling over in the trenches, so ill they could not move.

John DeWitt was among the victims.

In a letter home on May 19—a week before the gas attack—my grandfather mentioned his annoyance at fleas everywhere. Fleas meant the perpetrators of trench fever, lice, were there as well. I imagine in the trenches, scratching away, he would have been unlikely to know the difference, or care, for that matter.

Lice were as much a part of life in the trenches as the mud.

"Cooties" (fleas), oh yes, we are well acquainted. I think I could find one or two now if I were to look. I take a bath and a change of underwear at least once a week but it is almost impossible to get rid of them.

The fleas and lice, whose breeding thrived in the squalid living conditions in the trenches would bring the 168th briefly to its knees.

Life amid the filth had become so routine my grandfather seemed to me to be proud that he maintained such high standards of hygiene that he showered and changed his underwear once a week. I imagined him later in life, the always immaculately dressed small-town lawyer, turning to his wife and my grandmother Helen and telling her that he planned to bathe next week and, while he was at it, perhaps change his underwear as well.

It would not have flown.

By May 28, the day after the gas attacks, John DeWitt would have it too.

> *I am feeling better today and think I will be all okay by tomorrow. I had a touch of trench fever, which is quite prevalent.*

From my own research and my epidemiology and microbiology studies in medical school classes, I knew that there was no such thing as a "touch" of trench fever. It was debilitating to anyone who got it. There was no middle ground, just as I knew no one could become only "slightly" pregnant.

As always with John DeWitt and his letters home, "quite prevalent" was an understatement. Trench fever was rife in the ranks of the 168th.

To make matters far worse, the situation was complicated by the fact that its symptoms—the fever and the aching, among others—were similar to those brought on by inhaling the lethal phosgene. The medical staff, already overworked by the gas attack, were under great pressure. Anyone with a fever was sent to the hospital. Those suffering from inhaling the gas would die. Those with trench fever would recover in no more than five days, but they would be lost for much needed patrolling until then.

That dilemma would be gut-wrenching for the doctors. Soldiers too.

As the day following the gas attack progressed, "men who thought they were only slightly gassed developed serious symptoms as a result of the insidious effects of the phosgene and had to be taken to the rear," John Taber reported.

Some of the 168th companies were at less than half strength, ailing from either the gas or trench fever.

Taber recalled:

> *The effects of the gas were everywhere apparent. Everything was dead. Animal and vegetable life alike had been killed by the fumes. Messenger pigeons lay in their baskets; rats, swollen and distended, were stretched out in the trenches and dugouts; and the few stray cats which had made their homes in the vicinity had suffered a similar extinction. The whole area looked as if it had been visited by a killing frost-leaves and grass were seared and yellow—and over all hung the sweet, musty odor of phosgene that lingered most persistently in the low places and deep trenches.*

With the fighting at Belleau Wood just beginning and its positive outcome still unknown, and the 168th recoiling from the gas and trench fever, *The Stars and Stripes* ran a small front-page, one-column article celebrating a certain anniversary.

Tucked below the crease of its June 7, 1918 issue, was the headline:

A.E.F's Birthday Comes Tomorrow; Now A Year Old

> *A year ago tomorrow the vanguard of the A.E.F. landed at Liverpool.*
>
> *On June 8, 1917, General Pershing and his staff set foot on English soil. Late in the afternoon on June 13, the were welcomed at the gates of Paris by such a moving, spontaneous, tumultuous greeting from the people of the city as the will remember all the days of their lives, such a welcome, probably, as they cannot know again until the war is done and the A.E. F. goes home.*

I could think only of the welcoming committees of lice and fleas and God knows what else that greeted my Grandfather in Badonvillers and Ville Negre—and of the despicable conditions that allowed these vermin to thrive.

I thought of the old saw about how the lack of a nail prompted, in turn, the loss of a shoe, a horse, a man, and ultimately, a war. It seemed to be eminently applicable to the situation—an ominous warning that the smallest of things can spark the direst of consequences.

Lice, tiny specs carrying disease, could decimate an army.

The first case of what would become known as trench fever emerged in 1915 when a British medical officer reported a soldier who was suffering from fever, headache, dizziness, and shin pain. Within months, additional cases were reported in front line troops.

The causes of trench fever would not be understood for two more years.

No government effort would be worthy of its name if it weren't bogged down by bureaucracy. Even then. In 1917, the British formed the British Expeditionary Force Pyrexia of Unknown Origin Enquiry Sub-Committee. Not to be outdone, the Americans created the Medical Research Committee of the American Red Cross.

The Americans would find that lice were the perpetrators of trench fever and the British would show that scratching soldiers would open their skin and unintentionally rub the louse's excrement into their bloodstream. With it came rickettsia, the disease-causing bacteria.

While scientists by 1917 understood the origins and mechanisms of disease, no one on either side of the trenches could eliminate the base cause—the filth and the squalidness of the trenches that continued to breed lice.

I found the thought intriguing in an uneasy way. The louse, or more specifically its feces, had an unprecedented effect on armies of both sides. More than 1 million troops, German and Allied, were infected, unable to fight for days because of the resultant headache, dizziness, back ache, and what was described as an odd pain and stiffness in soldiers' legs, particularly their shins.

Treatment for trench fever was spotty and ineffective. Doctors tried quinine because it had worked against malaria. They tried a drug named Salvarsan because it appeared to work against syphilis. Nothing was effective.

My grandfather and the rest of the 168th were fortunate to have only come down with trench fever from their lice. Louse-borne typhus would kill an estimated two to three million soldiers and civilians on the Eastern Front—which stretched from the Baltic Sea in the north to the Black Sea in the south.

My own skin began to crawl imagining a phantom louse in my home.

As the month of June progressed, my indefatigable Grampa never mentioned trench fever again in any letter home.

Fighting in June 1918 was heavy. The war was reaching the point that for the Americans, fighting would always be heavy. "While our supremacy in No Man's Land was hotly contested, it was never seriously threatened, although the regiment lost a number of prisoners one day when one of our patrols clashed with the enemy," John Taber wrote of the 168th's active June.

With the fighting intense, John DeWitt was busy.

He was also homesick.

On June 2, he'd write home, complaining not of trench fever or gas, but of the number of letters he had to answer:

> *Everything is going lovely only I have an awful bunch of letters to write. Gee, but Rose F. certainly wrote me a very nice letter and I was certainly glad to get it and will answer it soon. Tot's letter was very newsy and interesting, just like having a little chat with her. The letter from the girl from Messco was also very cheery and newsy, like a breath of air from Messco.*

I noticed a change in his demeanor, though. Perhaps a bit of war-weariness was setting in. He was no longer excited about the shells and patrols, which had become so routine they had lost their glow, their intriguing specialness that gave him a chance to modestly crow a bit about what he was involved in.

> *Every time I write it seems as though there is less to write*

He echoed the sentiment on June 18:

> *I couldn't think of any more to write so I quit*

The 168th would be relieved from its duties on the front on June 20 and have a chance to rest. They had been under frequent artillery attack for weeks. Once relieved, the men would head for a rest at Neufmaisons, then on to Baccarat.

After that, "then farewell to Lorraine and its kindly people," John Taber would write.

On June 28, my grandfather wrote of the move.

> *Yes, we have moved and have lit in one spot for a few days. At least we have done a lot of traveling including automobiles, train and on foot. I have enjoyed it immensely. We have certainly seen some wonderful scenery again. We are in a much prettier and richer part of the country. The opportunity also presented itself of seeing a large city or two. We are enjoying a rest after our lengthy stay in the trenches. Our stay is a record so far, I believe. It sure seems good to get back where you can chase around without your "tin hat" or gas masks once more. Where you can go to bed without expecting or being called out at any moment by a gas or some other alarm. Where you can go to bed and take off most of your clothes.*

July would be a difficult month—a very difficult month that would culminate, as Taber would describe it, with "the tragic thirtieth."

In Iowa, after more than a year of war, things had changed since Grampa had been home.

TWENTY-ONE

AS MY GRANDFATHER sat back and relished his brief break in Neufmaisons, he was blissfully unaware that the fighting just ended in Lorraine had been mild compared with what awaited the 168th that summer in Champagne-Marne, Aisne-Marne, and St. Mihiel.

On July 9, he wrote home announcing he was heading out again. I was struck by his mention of friends, obviously Council Bluffs boys his mother would know. His affection and concern for them was obvious.

> *July 9, 1918*
> *[This letter was mailed by an officer from Texas in New York City on his way home. There was no censor.]*
>
> *Dearest Mother o' mine,*
>
> *Just a few lines to you in care of one of our Lieutenants who is going back.*
>
> *I am just fine in all respects, best of health and good spirits and all okay.*
>
> *Most of the boys are all okay also, Don, Ted, Phil, John Thomas, Poston and etc. Lieutenant PA Lainson is in command now and most of the Company are greatly pleased.*

> *You know we have left the vicinity of Baccarat and are at present in reserve in back of the big front, just where I can't say.*

By the time my grandfather reached that "big front," many of the men of the 168th would be in peril—mourning friends and thankful to be alive.

Some 4,000 miles away, there was another front developing, of all places, back home in Iowa, where things had grown contentious. Gone from Council Bluffs for close to a year by July 1918, my grandfather might not have recognized the growing tensions in his old stomping grounds.

The summer of 1918 was not a good time to be of German heritage in Iowa, or in the United States.

Anti-German sentiment had reached a peak in a state with a large population of German-Americans. It was not complicated to see why. Young men from Council Bluffs and across the state and country were being killed with great regularity in France. The enemy killing them, the Germans, were reviled.

As I learned more about the bloody summer combat in France, I began to wonder how my grandfather's always glowingly optimistic letters home were received by his parents and sisters. Despite his best intentions to avoid mentioning death, hardship, or danger, his mother and father must have known by the summer of 1918 that their son was in a precarious situation and would be until the war was over.

In the summer of 1918, no one knew when that would be.

By the time the war ended on November 11, some 4,088 Iowans would be dead. More would die later from injuries and the ravages of the Spanish flu. Forty-four soldiers who died were from the small city of Council Bluffs, a conspicuous amount of young men from a place with a population of 36,000. Many would have been high school classmates and perhaps friends or acquaintances of my grandfather.

And by the time the 168th went through training and crossing over to France, many more men who would later die would have become friends with the affable John DeWitt.

Reading about the men who died I noticed how many didn't actually die on the battlefield directly from bombs or bullets, but died later. It made me think, as an orthopaedic surgeon, about the tools we have now that didn't exist then and how many of those lives could be saved today.

Soldiers are trained now to stop major hemorrhage with a tourniquet. Many, if not all, have those in their packs. That prevents life threatening bleeding from a single extremity wound.

Present day evacuation gets wounded soldiers quickly to nearby field hospitals where medical teams can stop bleeding, stabilize fractures, and quickly replace fluids to stabilize blood pressure.

They are quickly transported to major medical centers for definitive surgery.

But the big one is antibiotics. Immediate "prophylactic" antibiotics that can prevent infection. The number of soldiers that must have died from "blood poisoning" or sepsis (life ending infections spread throughout the entire body) must have been staggering. Antibiotics to treat lungs with pneumonia damaged from "poison gas" would have saved thousands.

What a shame.

For his family back in Council Bluffs, it would have been hard to ignore the obituaries in the *Daily Nonpariel*. To make the losses more noticeable, mothers of soldiers killed in

France, at Woodrow Wilson's insistence, would begin in May 1918 wearing black armbands bearing a gilt star to announce their loss.

Such announcements would have been glaring, even for a family who seemed to have elevated the act of denial to an artform. I suspect the entire DeWitt family was genetically disinclined to delve in darkness, believing that that by not mentioning death or injury, they would avoid it.

By the time my grandfather was packing up and leaving Lorraine in June 1918, the brutality of the war was common knowledge in Council Bluffs and across the state and country.

It must have been excruciating for my grandfather's family to get through each day without thinking of the thin odds of seeing their oldest son again.

For many Americans in 1918, more than a year into the war, it was becoming easier to dislike Germans—and their German-American neighbors would pay a price. In Iowa the enmity was especially harsh, culminating in May 1918, when Governor William F. Harding announced new laws that, among other things, made speaking German in public illegal.

I had grown up fifty years later in Ida Grove, Iowa, a small town smack dab between the similarly small towns of Schleswig and Holstein, whose German heritage was thick, like many towns in the state. The idea of anti-German feelings and the violence that accompanied them seemed very strange to me when I learned of it, and as a boy I was unaware of it.

Knowing my Grampa and his beliefs, I am certain no one from his family would have felt anything but sympathy for their German neighbors. In all likelihood, his Irish immigrant mother and father—my great-grandparents—would have tried to help anyone being harassed. Good Catholics, sensible and kind people, such discrimination would have been an anathema to them.

As I learned, anti-Irish sentiment had been (and perhaps even still was) quite prevalent and I'm sure they would have sympathized with their German neighbors.

Before the new laws in Iowa, there were other signs that made it easier to scapegoat German-Americans.

Newspaper readers across Iowa—and across the county—were often cajoled to buy Liberty Bonds to raise money for the war effort through advertisements like the one that appeared in the Decorah, Iowa, *Public Opinion* in April 1918. John DeWitt's mother most likely read the same advertisement in the *Daily Nonpariel*.

> *The War Is Being Fought in Europe,*
>
> *But It Must be Won right Here at Home*
>
> *If the people of the earth are not to become toiling millions for the Prussian Junkers and the Prussians Krupps, if they are not to be toiling slaves at the mercy of a German Kaiser's will, Prussianism must be driven back to within its own borders and kept there.*
>
> *We're fighting for the safety and liberty of our children, our homes, our country.*
>
> *No Price is too great to pay for our Victory!*

On May 23, 1918—four days before the 163rd Infantry was nearly wiped out in the German gas attack—Iowa Governor Harding signed what became known as the Babel Proclamation, to "bring about peace, quiet, and harmony among our people."

It had the opposite effect among an increasingly angry public, where residents publicly burned German books and painted German-American businesses, churches, and homes yellow. German churches were vandalized, and in some cases, burned. German speakers were set on by mobs.

The Babel Proclamation made it illegal to speak anything but English in schools, on trains, in churches—even on party-line telephone calls. In a speech to the Des Moines chamber of commerce, Harding said that "those who insist upon praying in some other language are wasting their time, for the good Lord up above is now listening for the voice in English."

I wondered how John DeWitt and his family felt about that. Devout Catholics, they would have been attending weekly Masses celebrated in Latin.

Other Midwestern states followed suit and by the end of the war, some 18,000 people were charged under new anti-German laws, including four women in Scott County, Iowa, who were fined $250 for speaking German over the phone.

The anti-German hysteria in Iowa was set against a backdrop of nation-wide animosity—spurred on by the likes of former president Theodore Roosevelt, who noted that "hyphenated Americans like German-Americans should leave the country."

The 1918 Sedition Act called for fines of up to $10,000 and prison sentences of up to 20 years for insults directed at the U.S Government, flag, Constitution, or military. The vitriol led some citizens to force those they identified as immigrants to fly the American flag and buy Liberty Bonds as a show of support for American effort in the war.

About 6,000 Sedition Act offenders were arrested; some were not released until 1920.

My grandfather was a patriotic man whose values and love of his country led him to drop his plans to attend medical school and enlist. He did not simply pay lip service to his army obligation, but he took on a job that would very possibly kill him.

He was immensely proud of his service.

For the rest of his life he remained an ardent Republican and supporter of conservative causes. I have no doubt he would have seen both the Babel Proclamation and the Sedition Act as necessary. He would have wasted no time in cynical thoughts about the need for such legislation or its applications.

As I read more about the deaths of his Council Bluffs friends and his comrades from the 168th, I wondered how often over the course of his long life he might have lamented their passing. He never spoke of that to me when I was a child visiting him in Griswold.

I pored over a list of men from Council Bluffs who had died in France. I could not help but think that each had likely gone through training with my grandfather at Camp Dodge and Camp Mills and had made the ill-fated Atlantic crossing on the *President Grant*.

Each, like my grandfather, had his own dreams.

John DeWitt, running messages in what was considered an inevitably fatal job, made it home. Some of his friends and comrades from Council Bluffs did not.

I was chilled by the role of fate in their lives, or luck good and bad.

I wondered if Grampa ever thought about his charmed life in France. I wondered how often he thought of his dead friends buried in Council Bluffs.

Had he known Bryant Badger, killed on September 12, 1918, by machine gun fire near Fliery?

Did he go to high school with Ralph W. Davis, wounded at the beginning of the Champagne defense in July while standing at his post in the trench before dying at a camp hospital?

Had he hung out with David Faulk, who died of wounds received in action on November 1, 1918?

Or perhaps he knew Thomas E. Langan, who in the last advance of his company was slightly wounded only to die of pneumonia in a hospital after the Armistice was signed.

Did he know Edwin Lindsay, who volunteered to repair telephone wires under heavy fire on June 20, 1918, was wounded and died later at a hospital on July 4?

My grandfather was surrounded by ghosts. And though he never spoke of them that I'm aware of to his children, my mother and Uncle Jack, I imagine he drew strength and comfort from the time they all shared in a common sacrifice for the good of America.

Did he think of them often?

I suspect so.

TWENTY-TWO

THE MEN OF the 168th began July 1918 knowing they were about to be thrust into combat unlike anything they'd seen before. By mid-July the promise came true, with the 168th—and John DeWitt—called on to be a part of a massive effort thrown by the Allies against what would prove to be the last large German offensive of the war.

July 1918 was harsh, deadly, and exhausting.

On July 5, *The Stars and Stripes,* in a boxed article at the top of the front page, urged on American troops.

> *On this anniversary of our independence, the officers and men of the American Expeditionary Forces on the battlefields of France renew their pledges of fealty and devotion to our cause and country. The resolve of our forefathers that all men and all people shall be free is their resolve. It is quickened by sympathy for an invaded people of kindred ideas and the war challenges of an arrogant enemy. It is fortified by the united support of the American people.*

I'm certain the paper's editors printed the story that appeared below the Independence Day call to action as a lighthearted diversion from what was about to befall the soldiers reading it. As I scrolled down the front page, another article caught my eye, and I laughed. As he prepared for combat, my grandfather would no doubt have sought out a priest and gone to confession.

> ***Dolan's Confession Lengthy Process***
>
> *Did you ever go looking up your sins in an English-French dictionary? Take it from Private Edward Dolan of the Engineers—it's a tough job.*
>
> *Private Dolan had wanted to go to confession for a long while. He finally found a priest who was stationed near the particular part of the front which was his habitat at the time. The priest couldn't talk English and Dolan couldn't talk French, but he confessed just the same.*
>
> *Here's how. The priest had a little French-English dictionary. He lent it to Private Dolan, who looked through it until he found some of his sins listed.*
>
> *It took Private Dolan about two hours to make his confession, and he's not a particularly sinful member of the A.E.F at that.*

There was little humor in what the Americans faced in July 1918.

That month, as the Germans began their next assault, part of the faltering Spring offensive, they had lost more than 600,000 casualties. After four years of fighting, there were no more reserves to step up and replace the dead and disabled. Americans and their French and British allies were dying in great numbers too, but they were gaining control.

Raymond Tomkins wrote of the shift in momentum in *The Story of the Rainbow Division,* and of a new and chilling desperation among the Germans about facing the Americans.

> *There was looming up in the German army a feeling of terror of these quick, forward-moving men in olive-drab, who were not afraid even of the wonderful German machine-guns, but who dived and wriggled toward them and were suddenly all around them in desperate little rings.*
>
> *German gunners were being chained to their guns; it was becoming necessary. And since men at bay will always fight for their lives, the fights around the machine-gun nests were nearly always fights to the death.*

German morale was dropping. The Americans, now combat-hardened veterans, were arriving at the front in increasing numbers. By July, Allied troops outnumbered the Germans on the Western Front.

As part of their final thrust that weakened the German army, the Allies had begun a two-pronged attack on either side of the city of Reims on July 15.

German commanders had predicted the assault would deal a death blow to the Allies and their new American friends.

The Allies, bolstered by 85,000 combat-experienced Americans, had other ideas.

Met by aggressive, unrelenting resistance and counterattacks by French, British, American, and Italian troops, the grand German plan began to falter and bog down.

The balance of power began to shift in favor of the Allies.

On July 15, my grandfather would find himself in Suippes, a small village along the Western Front that had seen more than its share of hardship. In the first months of the war, the region in which Suippes sat had been pummeled. In four years, the front lines had barely moved.

John Ryder DeWitt's actions in Suippes that day would change the course of the war for him. What I learned about his actions under fire that day in Suippes—more than his letters home, my research, my memories of him, and the recollections of family members—would indelibly define the man I had been looking for.

In early July, anticipating the German strike, the 168th had been ordered to move to Suippes and made the 20-kilometer march on a black night in a cold and steady drizzle. The fighting was all around them.

John Taber described the march:

> *It was so dark that it was almost impossible to see one's file leader, and the column progressed with accordion-like jerks which added immeasurably to the discomfort of a difficult enough march. The blackness of the night intensified the brilliance of the gun flashes that played like heat lightning along the horizon as the regiment once more neared the front.*

By the time the German assault began shortly after midnight on July 15, Suippes had become desolate, etched by a labyrinth of trenches captured from the Germans in what had been one of the most bitterly contested battlegrounds of the war. The French had on three different occasions assaulted German lines in the area—in February, March, and September of 1915, and in April 1917. More soldiers had died there per kilometer than any other place on the front.

John Taber described the region poetically.

Here and there stood the lonely graves of heroes fallen for La Patrie in the battles which had raged back and forth over this land. And over all was the brilliant splash of millions of poppies, blood-red, vivid against the glistening white of the chalk.

The poppies were a big deal to Grampa. He wore one every Veterans day.

In Suippes, the Americans were fighting alongside the French Fourth Army, under the command of Henri Gouraud, a one-armed general much beloved and respected by his troops. John Taber referred to Gouraud, who had lost his arm from a combat injury in 1915, as a "genius."

On July 7, Gouraud addressed his troops and the Americans. Taber was enthralled by his speech. "Even now one thrills at the reading of it, and it can be imagined what was the moral effect at the time on soldiers who realized that they were holding in their hands the destiny of nations."

My grandfather likely heard Gouraud's inspiring oration. By then, he was in the thick of it and there was no turning back. A week later he would prove his mettle.

Taber paraphrased Gouraud's address:

> *We may be attacked at any moment. You all know that a defensive battle was never engaged under more favorable conditions. We are awake and on our guard. We are powerfully reinforced with infantry and artillery. You will fight on a terrain which you have transformed by your labor and perseverance into a redoubtable fortress, an invincible fortress if all its entrances are well guarded.*
>
> *The bombardment will be terrible; you will face it without weakness; the assault will be fierce in clouds of smoke, dust, and gas; but your position and your armament are formidable. In your breasts beat the brave and strong hearts of free men.*

> *None shall glance to the rear; none shall yield a step. Each shall have but one thought; to kill, to kill many, until they shall have had enough.*
>
> *Therefore, your General says to you: "You will break this assault, and it will be a happy day."*

Gouraud was remarkably prescient.

The general had also determined, correctly, that the Germans would attack on the 15th, to take advantage of what they hoped would be French lassitude following Bastille Day celebrations and heavy drinking the day before. The Americans had been given Bastille Days off as well, and the men from Iowa had played a raucous game of soccer against the French behind the trenches that afternoon—on a field John Taber noted "that ten hours later was ploughed deep with enemy high explosive."

The German bombardment, described in one account as an "avalanche" began shortly after midnight along a 42-mile-long front and would last for four hours. That was only the beginning.

The History of the Rainbow Division described the initial onslaught:

> *There was death and destruction in the very air; it seemed to be reaching out with hungry, clutching hands, sweeping victims in; the sky swished and swirled like a hurricane, bringing a rain that burst with a red crash when it landed, and the clean night breeze became a deadly draft of poisonous gas.*

For my grandfather, the chaos would have been immutable. He did not waver and continued to deliver messages under fire. That was, after all, what he had trained for. Delivering messages was his duty. Bombs and shells fell all night long on both the front fighting lines and rear areas, including field hospitals. As light grew with the dawn, circling German airplanes strafed the Allied troops with machine-gun fire and sprays of steel darts called flechettes, which were essentially pencil-sized short steel rods with a sharp point at one end, and fins at the other. Originally invented by the Italians in 1911–1912, they were first used by the French in 1914, although they were also later used by the British and Germans. Troops feared them, in a sense because they were wildly inaccurate and cause "gruesome mutilations."

German guns were accurate and deadly. John Taber recounted his men watching in horror as two American artillery batteries received direct hits and the crews blown to pieces.

The barrage was unrelenting. Taber wrote:

> *As in the grasp of a great hurricane that tears and pulls, the trees above them were being twisted and battered. Men were torn and blown to atoms before the eyes of their comrades. White chalk was spurting up in cloudy geysers. A platoon of E Company was severely hit when the barrage swept over its trench. Lieutenant Doolittle and forty per cent of his men were struck in ten minutes time, and it was a miracle that any of them escaped.*

Casualties were high during the first hours of the assault, so much so that medical stations were overwhelmed, unable to care for the wounded and dying men brought in by stretcher-bearers. In the next few days casualties were, to use Taber's description, "severe"—all due to the heavy shelling.

Seventy-six men of the 168th were killed and 237 wounded in the first days of the attack.

Through this chaos and Taber's artful description of the battle, I sensed my grandfather emerge. There were communication problems. Telephone and telegraph wires were quickly blown to shreds.

The runners stepped up.

> *The battalion commanders were having a trying experience in getting information from their companies and relaying it back to Regimental Headquarters. All the wires so carefully strung went down the first minute, and the T. P. S. [field telephone] was useless in such a storm. The signal men performed prodigies of work in their futile efforts to maintain the communications. Sometimes the line would go out in the middle of a word, and a man would vanish without order to repair it so that the sentence might be finished. One base line was spliced no less than forty-three times during the bombardment, but to no avail. The matter resolved itself into the use of runners, and this was not the most satisfactory of means on shell-swept roads and in caving trenches. But in spite of the peril, these brave messengers persisted and some of them got through.*

John DeWitt persisted, certainly. He stepped up without hesitation.

Reading Taber's description of the assault, I found a passage that brought me full circle—back to what sparked me to begin my search to learn as much as I could about my grandfather's war experiences.

It was an account of Billy Schupp's death that echoed the fragile and yellowed *Stars and Stripes* article and my grandfather's note to me in 1972—the one I did not see until 2020.

Taber's description was a confirmation of the very thing that had started me on my journey. But that was not all. The various items I had been assembling, trying to make sense of John DeWitt's time in the army, suddenly snapped together like the final piece in a jigsaw puzzle when I found another item tucked away on the back of a letter: a memorandum from an officer that would give meaning to my project and eliminate any ambiguity about the war and my grandfather's role in it.

But first I read Taber's account of Billy Schupp's demise. Schupp and Boysen were trench-runners. They were from Council Bluffs. My grandfather knew them and they shared the same duties. They were all interchangeable. My grandfather could have easily been in their place that day.

Taber recalled:

> *Billy Schupp and Fred Boysen started from Lieutenant Lainson's P. C. with a message for Major Brewer giving the details of L Company's situation. When they had got out about a hundred yards, Schupp turned and said something to Boysen, who was five feet behind, but the roar was so great that he was not heard. A few steps further, and a German shell burst in the boyau. When Boysen came to, he was lying crosswise in the trench with the mangled body of Schupp on top of him. He lifted him off and turned him over once or twice to make sure that he was not alive, and then, reaching in the breast pocket of his comrade, took out the message and started ahead. He knew that he himself had been hit in the leg, but was still too dazed from the explosion to realize how badly; and somehow he managed to stumble along until another runner overtook him and helped him to Battalion*

> *Headquarters. There he delivered his message and told of the fate of Schupp. Then he started to pull himself up the steep flight of steps.*
>
> *"Where are you going", he was asked.*
>
> *"Why, to get my buddy, of course", he replied. But his weakened body could carry him no farther, and he sank at the feet of the men who would have restrained him.*
>
> *The runners were not alone in the open. The stretcher bearers, volunteers for the most part, were searching for wounded men in the woods and in the crumbling trenches. In the midst of the Hell and destruction, never stopping to dodge, no matter how close the shell, they carried their burdens to shelter or to the aid stations. Many were felled, but there were always others ready to fill the gaps and to carry on with the same rare courage. In the heavily shelled Company K sector, four were killed by one shell, only the wounded man they were shouldering escaping death. It was men like these, exposed to all the dangers of the battle and expecting none of its rewards, who merit the greatest measure of praise.*

Five days later, July 20, my grandfather would write home. And for the first time since he began writing more than a year earlier, he came as close to describing the war as he had ever done.

> *I sure know what the hottest kind of fighting is in the worst way in history and, believe me, it is sure hell with a lot of extras thrown in.*
>
> *I suppose you have all been very much worried over your failure to hear from me but we have been so busy doing a lot of things that there has been no chance at all.*

We were in place to break the Boche advance, which started on July 14th. They sure gave us hell but they didn't get where we could use the bayonets on them, thanks to the extraordinary and wonderful work of the French and some Americans.

There was not a softer way to describe combat, nor a way to dance around the subject as he usually did.

He told his mother in that July 20 letter that he was lucky he had survived, a rare bit of candor from the reticent and protective son.

Thank the good Lord that I was spared this time

"It sure is good to know that a powerful drive of the huns was stopped at all points. It is also good to know we were a factor in it."

I had, in a way, begun my search for my grandfather's untold war experiences in July 1918. I entered the picture after my sister had discovered the letters packed away in boxes in our Uncle Jack's garage in 2020.

I thought again of his note to me:

October 17, 1972
To: Jack DeWitt, John Chase and any other interested persons

You have asked me about my war experiences.

I told you I was a Battalion runner, but I don't think it meant a great deal to you.

I recalled that there was an article in the Stars and Stripes about runners.

> *The other day Joel Boone brought in a book containing articles of the Stars and Stripes.*
>
> *I looked and found the above account.*
>
> *Al Boysen and Billy Schupp were members of my own Company L.*
>
> *They were company runners.*
>
> *I was located at battalion headquarters.*
>
> *Each company had two runners there.*
>
> *It was after the above described battle that I was recommended for a DFC (but it should have been DSC-Distinguished Service Cross)*
>
> *I was given a Division citation rather than the DSC.*
>
> *I thought you would be interested in reading same.*

Seeing that note had sparked me to begin my quest to make sense of the letters we had found. When I read the *Stars and Stripes* article for the first time in the summer of 2020, it seemed in a way nothing more than a distant account of a horrible event that had taken place a century before during a war I knew little about.

I would be shocked again when I pulled my grandfather's July 20 letter from the pile I had neatly arranged on my desk. I saw something I had not noticed before, even though I had read the letters many times.

> *After the censors sign off: We were at Suippes (look it up), not far from Chalons. Keep it quiet*

On the back of the July 20 letter I noticed something I had overlooked—the succinct recommendation from an officer that John DeWitt be awarded a medal for his actions on July 15. My grandfather seemed to have slipped the extra note into his letter after the censor had reviewed it.

That commendation was tucked away in the same manner my grandfather had tucked away his life in the army and at war. He had not necessarily hidden it. I could have easily discovered it earlier if I had been more diligent—in the same way I could have learned of his war experiences if I had seen his 1972 note.

That commendation would provide the details he tried to give me in 1972.

When I read the commendation, I was overcome by both a sense of irony and by the feeling my grandfather was talking to me.

July 26, 1918
From: Assistant Division Adjutant
42nd Division
To: Private John DeWitt
Company L
168 Infantry (through military channels)
Subject: COMMENDATION

I am directed by a Division Commander to inform you that your conduct on the occasion of the bombardment northeast of Suippes, July 15, 1918, when you carried important messages to your Company Commander at a time the trenches were shelled so violently you were compelled to take the exposed route over the top and although being slightly gassed, you insisted upon staying on duty, has been brought to his personal attention and he considers your performance of duty on this occasion worthy of the highest accommodation. He regards your actions, in

> *the face of the enemy, gallant and an example to your comrades in arms and characteristic of that splendid standard upon which the traditions of our military establishment are founded.*
>
> *James E. Thomas*
> *Captain*
> *HG Adjutant General*

If I had seen his 1972 note to me—or if I had been more interested—I would have known John Ryder DeWitt was a war hero—and very close to being a dead war hero.

The commendation would provide the epiphany that transformed my search and raised it to a level I had not expected.

This was the source of his remarks in his note to me in 1972, when he wrote: "It was after the above described battle that I was recommended for a DFC (but it should have been DSC-Distinguished Service Cross)I was given a Division citation rather than the DSC."

I would learn something else from my grandfather's next letter home, written on July 31.

The odds of him delivering messages, over the top and exposed to the shells and the strafing and the enemy snipers and escaping unscathed were astronomical.

One of his last lines to his mother in the July 20 letter made more sense when I read his July 31 letter.

> *I am in God's care and will probably be back all safe and sound when it is over.*

His July 31 letter was written from a hospital in Paris. John Ryder DeWitt's war was over.

TWENTY-THREE

MY GRANDFATHER, HOLDING back as usual, was being coy when he wrote home on July 20 to say he was fine. His actions in a fierce battle July 15 had come close to killing him. But he was alive, certainly, and in the context of what he had just been though, that could qualify as "fine."

He had not told his mother the entire story of what happened to him that day.

His July 31 letter, written from a hospital bed, would be more expansive. It included Captain Thomas's commendation and a scribbled note about where he had been. The remaining letters he wrote from France would continue to offer more details about what he had seen and experienced.

Reading that letter, I noticed something subtle but clear. His tone was changing. Hospitalized in Paris, my grandfather began to open up to his parents about the war, and about injuries—his own and those of his friends.

From that Paris hospital bed, Grampa wrote that he had a "wee" bit of shrapnel in his left leg, adding that he expected to be at the unnamed Paris hospital for only a day or two before returning to battle. He neglected to mention he had been gassed.

July 31, 1918
Paris

Dearest Mother o' mine,

I bet you were mighty surprised to see that I was writing you from Paris. I am here in an evacuation hospital, got here yesterday. Expect I will only be here a day or two more before they will send me some place else but a short time and I will be back with the Outfit.

Right here with me are two more fellows out of my Company, Elmer Poston and Chris Berthleson (who is a prince of a fellow, a real good friend of mine and from Sioux City). We all have slight flesh wounds. Thank the good Lord. I got a wee bit of shrapnel in my left thigh. Elmer got a bit in the right buttock and Chris got a machine gun bullet in the flesh of the right leg.

It was certainly a battle for fair. I suppose you know by this time we lost a lot of the boys but the greater part were only wounded.

After I wrote you last, we started on our way up here, traveling first by train, then hiking, then by trucks, some more hiking and then we were into it up against the Boche. Then it was a fight every step of the way. We certainly did give them hell but we also caught an awful lot of hell ourselves.

I have received better treatment from the time I was tagged to go to the hospital up until the present time than I have ever received before since I joined the Army. They certainly do treat you fine in the hospital, at least so far.

His assertion that he would soon be back in combat was wrong. He would not fight again, nor, I believe, have to begin each day worried about the consequences of delivering messages under fire or through a cloud of phosgene gas.

Was he vastly relieved?

I wondered when he knew he would not fight again. I wondered also if he had heard what the 168th had gone through as he recovered in his hospital bed.

On July 30, John Taber's "tragic 30th," the 168th had been severely tested.

While my grandfather lay in the hospital in Paris recovering from his wounds and gassing, the 168th was ordered to attack and capture the village of Nesles, north of Sergy.

The Germans knew what was coming and were prepared, setting up artillery and machine guns overlooking an open field through which the Iowans would have to pass to reach Nesles. Any men from the 168th who survived the direct artillery bombardment would be cut down by withering machine gun fire.

Taber reported that officers from the 168th knew the Germans would not cede Nesles without a "bitter fight."

The brutal combat to take Nesles, eventually won by the Americans, was bloody and chaotic. Battalion runners played a significant if exhausting role in the victory. Taber reported that runners from all three of the 168th's battalions performed "in a splendid manner."

Runners were killed, not unusual in such an assault where the American commanders were continually changing strategies to overcome the strong advantage held by the Germans. Messages were essential to a coordinated attack. Surviving runners were so exhausted from the effort that non-runners volunteered to deliver crucial messages.

A major's orderly, a man not usually called on to take up arms, stepped up after two runners were killed. He was not dissuaded by warnings that he would not make it very far along a path through the field that was being raked with German machine gun fire. He took a scribbled message from an officer and went, nonetheless. Still clutching his message, he was shot through his heart and died immediately. A private running behind him, removed the message from the dead orderly's hand and delivered it.

Another runner was shot in the face. A bullet clipped off part of his tongue after it passed through his cheek, leaving a gaping hole. His ear was hanging by a thin shred of skin, and he was bleeding profusely. He was guided to the medical station by another soldier who had lost a finger.

Twenty-five officers and 462 men from the 168th were killed, wounded, and gassed, according to John Taber.

There is no doubt John DeWitt would have been in the middle of the fight.

Being wounded and hospitalized in Paris on July 30, 1918 was a universe away from where John DeWitt had been one year before, when the jubilant new recruit, about to turn twenty-one years old in a month, wrote his first letter home:

> *Everything is just fine here, all okay and everything plenty work and very little time to write. Will have to make this short and sweet. We started to drill Monday and it's a drill too, believe me, our two weeks or so of ease sure softened me up.*
>
> *It is the same old story here, day in and day out. Went to church last Sunday, sure was nice. They have been giving us some new equipment today, belts and bayonets and first aid pack.*

It had been a remarkable year.

In July 1917 my grandfather had been marching with wooden rifles and training in dry, symmetrical trenches cut into the hard soil of Camp Dodge. There was no mud, no trench fever or trench foot. There were no nightly artillery barrages or messages to deliver while ducking sniper fire. Training was not easy, to be sure, but a year before he wrote from that hospital in Paris, my grandfather's life had been mostly patriotic fervor, parades, and near antiseptic hope unsullied by death and disease and carnage.

A year later he was in a hospital bed in France, having survived a harrowing Atlantic crossing, a brutal winter, the fetid life of the trenches, increasingly lethal and frequent gas attacks, and daily brushes with death—his own and those of his friends.

His letter from the Paris hospital bed was more frank than any he had written.

This sudden expansiveness to his parents had begun after the battle on July 15, his final fight.

In his July 20 letter, he had at last broken his unspoken rule that he would never write of the danger of what he had been doing. He told his mother for the first time he had almost been killed. Then, he had ignored regulations—something he had likely never done by sneaking in the additional information of where he was and Captain Thomas's commendation.

It dawned on me that while he was fighting, death—his death specifically—was not an event he chose to honor or acknowledge by writing about it. He clearly did not want to stare at the word written in a letter to his family.

In the hospital, when it became clear he would not be sent back into combat, he was freed from his self-imposed censorship. It was only then that he could acknowledge, yes, he had been doing things that could have easily gotten him killed.

In the hospital in August, he must have sensed the war was winding down as the Americans began to insert themselves in the Allied effort. He must have seen that victory was in sight. Indeed, the Armistice would arrive in November. Grampa must have felt safe, perhaps he even began to dream about returning home in one piece, alive.

He must have felt it was time to begin hinting at some of the things he had been doing—the horrible things he had seen and been through.

July 1918 was the turning point in the war, the month the Americans began to assert themselves and take the offensive aggressively and successfully against the weakening Germans. The Americans brought the war to the Germans and the Germans recoiled. John DeWitt was right there with them and came within a hair's breadth of being killed.

For John Ryder DeWitt—my garrulous, patriotic, daring and above all else, modest grandfather—the man who never mentioned he had served in one of the most dangerous jobs in the army—the war ended in a hospital bed in Paris at the end of July, 1918.

Once I had learned enough about the hard-won and bloody American advances in July 1918, and once I had digested the clues of my grandfather's last, heroic actions in combat, I was immensely proud of him, of course. But I began to wonder about him. A question emerged after I learned more about what he had done in July 1918. I tried to reconcile that new information about his near-death in combat—and the heroism that prompted it—with the old man I had known.

In the fifty-five Julys he spent after the war, did he ever stop and offer a prayer of thanks for his survival? On his birthdays in the ensuing years did he reflect on the grace and good luck that gave him his long and fruitful life? Did he offer a Hail Mary, perhaps, for his blessings, for escaping what many of his comrades did not?

I believe he did.

In the thick of it, with a rare bit of time on his hands to write and explain what he'd gone through, my grandfather's July 20 letter was filled with more frankness—rich hints and easily deciphered details—than any he had written since his first letter from Camp Dodge just over a year before.

He had been in combat, had survived and was grateful for it, he wrote his mother. He concluded, as he always did in his letters, with a reassurance.

> *I am just fine and in the best of health and okay in all respects.*

Perhaps for the first time since he had arrived in France, he began to think about returning to Iowa and moving on with his life. He must have felt extraordinary, and proud, especially after a year wondering each time he delivered a message or went to sleep in a trench, if he would be killed by a sniper's bullet, an artillery blast, or phosgene gas.

From April when he began running messages until he was wounded in July, my grandfather would see more than his share of combat and death—and he would become inured to it. During his months in combat, though, he never mentioned the details to his mother.

MY GRANDFATHER would enjoy a profusion of auspicious, life-affirming events in the fifty-five years he lived after July 15, 1918, a day he came very close to being killed. His first such blessing was his own survival. That he had stayed alive was close to miraculous, even for the charmed soon-to-be 22-year old. The fact he was in one piece and able to breathe clearly came after his karmic good luck inserted itself once again.

Back in Iowa after the war, my grandfather would move on from the job at Messco he seemed to love. He'd exchange his dream of medical school for a chance to study law at Creighton University across the river from Council Bluffs in Omaha. He would begin a prosperous and long law practice in Griswold. He would meet and marry Helen Brennan and start a family—my mother Maribeth and my Uncle Jack. He would watch his grandchildren grow. He played golf, supported Republican politics, smoked cigars and ate enough to expand an already ample waistline. He made friends easily.

My grandfather relished life and helped form an American Legion post. He did not carry the darker side of what he had gone through with him openly, if at all. As far as I know, he never had nightmares, though what he had gone through had been fertile grounds for producing them.

He was proud of his service, though not given to windy orations of his deeds.

He never mentioned his extraordinary life in the trenches to me until his note in 1972, the year before he died—and I was not aware that he did until 2020.

Still, if my grandfather was given to sentiment or nostalgia, I have no doubt July 1918 held a special place in his heart. It was a watershed month, not only for him but for the men of the 168th, the Rainbow Division, and the American Expeditionary Force.

He had done his share.

TWENTY-FOUR

ONE MONTH REMOVED from the day he came so close to dying, John DeWitt found himself a patient at the large Base Hospital # 8 in the village of Savenay, in western France.

By then, the loose-fitting Red Cross pajamas my grandfather wore were perfect to accommodate his growing girth. If he had to wear his uniform for any occasion, it certainly would have been very snug, buttons close to popping. The man's passion for food and eating as much of it as possible, even under the stress of combat, came into full bloom in Savenay, where daily life was predictable.

He was safe, clean, and full, his remarkable military journey nearing an end. In his letters home there were signs of boredom—an alien and long-missing emotion after the year he had been through.

August 16, 1918
Base hospital #8
Savenay

Dearest Mother o' mine,

Well how is everybody at home today? The correct answer is "just fine."

I feel pretty good this morning but that is about all. I went to Mass this morning, Assumption Thursday. It is customary in the states and Canada to celebrate it on the following Sunday for local reasons. In France, in particular, and most of the European countries, it is celebrated on the day proper. In France, it is also a Civil holiday. There is nothing new around these parts. No mail arrived yet for one thing or no pay either but we should worry? I see, by the papers which we get, that some real American casualty lists have at last been published. Did you see my name in any of them or were you notified that I had been wounded?

It is possible that the fellows sleeping on each side of me are both going back to the states because of their wounds. One of them is from Panama, Iowa. His name is Eugene Cain. I told him, if on his return he is discharged or gets a furlough and goes through the Bluffs, to look you up if possible. He may write you.

Today is a beautiful sunshiny day, a regular French summer day. The French summers are not near as hot as ours. Old fashioned Dutch mills are very numerous. They certainly look a way off on a hilltop going round and round.

[a diagram of the windmill]

Well Mother dear, I don't know anything else to write of interest so will close. Loads and loads of love to one and all.

Base Hospital # 8 at Savenay, as were other so-called base hospitals, was the last stop along a system of medical triage for wounded soldiers that American and British medical staffs had developed and improved over the years of the war.

Medical care for wounded soldiers began on the battlefield, where the main emphasis was to get wounded men to safety and medical care as quickly as possible. For stretcher-bearers, the trained volunteers assigned the onerous job, the job was dangerous. Stretcher-bearers underwent a 10-week training course is medical basics. Much like the messengers, stretcher-bearers went over the top to face what could be imminent death. Instead of messages, they carried with them medical supplies and a great deal of courage.

Once a wounded soldier reached relative safety, he would be transported to an evacuation hospital, a modern and highly efficient facility equipped with top-notch surgeons and operating theaters to care for the most seriously injured.

Surviving soldiers, out of danger and their health improving, would then be moved to a base hospital, which was usually either the final stop before returning to battle or heading home. By the war's end in November 1918, there were 238 base hospitals in France, a number that serves as testimony to the ravages of war.

With less than four months remaining in the war, John DeWitt, still irritated by the gas he had inhaled, was not ready to head back into combat.

He would be going home once his condition, not serious, improved.

It is clear that the triage system worked—injured soldiers who made it to the base hospital stage rarely died. Base Hospital #8 had 2,333 admissions in July 1918, with four deaths. In August, when my grandfather had settled in, there were 3,439 admissions and 15 deaths. In November, when the war ended, the hospital had 7,057 admissions and 31 deaths.

My grandfather's trip to Base Hospital #8 would have included all three phases of treatment. After being hit in the leg with shrapnel, he would have been treated as soon a possible, then stretchered off and transported to an evacuation hospital, most likely the one in Paris he wrote home from after his heroics on the battlefield.

It seems to me that my grandfather did not spend a great deal of time at the evacuation hospital. His shrapnel wound was minor, though the effects of inhaling gas continued to bother him.

He wrote home on August 7 to say that the effects of the gas was "hurting his eyes and lungs."

He was also continuing to be more introspective.

> *After a fellow goes through what I have just been through, he gets closer to God than ever before.*

His shrapnel wounds—caused by shards of torn metal from exploded bombs—would have been cleaned to remove any fragments, then flooded with antiseptic solutions such as boric acid and iodine. The dressing on his wound would have been changed frequently, which was often painful.

If John DeWitt needed treatment for gas, he could have received that offered by a typical base hospital in 1918, where nurses devised a mixture of "guaiacol, camphor, menthol, oil of thyme and eucalyptus" that would force patients to cough up mucous and the detritus caused by inflammation.

By 1918, caring for the wounded had become an efficient system designed to provide wounded soldiers with the best chance to survive not only their initial wounds, but also the infections and peripheral diseases that could kill.

That had not always been the case for soldiers wounded in battle.

During the Spanish American War some twenty years before, the Army's medical system was poorly organized, understaffed, and ill-prepared. As a result, wounded soldiers received inadequate care, then were sent to recover in poorly maintained and unsanitary hospitals, which led to a high rate of disease and deaths. Five times as many soldiers died from disease as were killed in combat.

An appalled public cried for reforms of the military medical services. By the time Woodrow Wilson declared war in April 1917, the Army Medical Department had improved substantially, though, like the Army itself, it was short-handed. At the beginning of the war the Medical Corps had 491 active-duty Army doctors. By the end of the war, there were 30,500 physicians—the result of an aggressive recruiting and training program. Before the end of the war in November 1918, more than 20,000 nurses would be serving on active duty.

Leading American medical schools—Johns Hopkins, Harvard, Western Reserve, Washington University, Duke, and the Universities of Kansas and Michigan—supported by the American Medical Association and the American College of Surgeons, set up and staffed a number of base hospitals that were moved to Europe to accommodate the growing number of casualties.

John DeWitt, his luck still hovering close by, certainly benefitted from the now thoroughly modern medical care.

Surgery techniques were sophisticated, and routine procedures to prevent sepsis were in place. Contributing to a wounded soldier's chance of survival was the fact that most had been immunized against tetanus and typhoid fever. Smallpox vaccinations were required, and intravenous fluid therapy was readily available, as were blood transfusions.

Of course, this modern and continuously improving system owed its efficiency to the stunning numbers of wounded soldiers who passed through it. Doctors had many chances to learn.

All was not rosy, of course. Large numbers of men were dying daily. As I continued my research into my grandfather's final months in Europe, I found a wrenching column in *The Stars and Stripes* by an unnamed reporter who had spent time observing the operations of an unidentified evacuation hospital around the same time John DeWitt was at Base Hospital #8 in Savenay.

The column appearing in the August 2, 1918, issue and was titled, "When the Wounded come In."

One vignette startled me. It reminded me of my grandfather's own sanitized letters home—though this scene took a darker turn.

> *He was smiling but pale when they wheeled him in—a black-haired youth of 20—and he was still smiling when they tenderly transferred him to a cot after the doctors had counted seven machine gun wounds, one in his ankle, three in his side, and three in his chest.*
>
> *When a Y.M.C.A. man brought writing paper through the ward he took a piece and asked for a pencil. An attendant found him dead half an hour later with the beginning of a letter in his hand:*
>
> *Dear Mother,*
>
> *We made an attack on the Germans today and drove them five miles. I was slightly wounded in the leg…*

Other stories captured the atmosphere and the attitudes, stoic and brimming with bravado, of the wounded.

Two soldiers lay side by side in an evacuation hospital. One was a browned red-headed doughboy with a broken arm. The other's head and face were bandaged so that only his mouth and chin were visible.

The doughboy raised on his pillow and surveyed his neighbor.

"Say, what outfit are you out of buddy?" he asked. "Your mug looks kind of familiar and I've been trying to place you."

"Company I, Infantry," said he of the bandaged head.

"So am I. Who the deuce are you?"

"I," said the other, "am the captain."

There was a bandage over his eye.

"Anything else the matter with you?" asked the surgeon who was standing beside his spot.

"Well, I got hit up there near the eye, but that ain't much. "

"Yes," persisted the surgeon, "but did you get hit anywhere else?"

Then he admitted that he had a broken arm, a broken leg, and a bullet in his side.

And the tireless and exhausting work of the doctors.

"I don't know," said the doctor, "I haven't been working so hard. I got up at 4 o'clock Monday morning, I had two hours sleep Wednesday, I had three hours sleep Friday, and Sunday morning at eight o'clock I went to bed and had a long rest—eight hours.

And finally, the pluck of the men.

Three wounds in five minutes—each of them worth a wound stripe—was one Infantryman's record.

"I got a machine gun bullet in the stomach," he explained. "It was about spent when it hit me. Fritz was shooting by indirect fire from long range. It just went through the skin and stuck there. I squeezed it out and was just putting it in my pocket when I got another in the leg. It went right in and right out and didn't hit the bone. I hadn't anymore begun to feel it when piece of shrapnel hit me in the same leg.

They certainly were after me but none of the wounds amounts to anything. I'll be back for more in three weeks.

Judging from my grandfather's hospital-bound letters home from Savenay, another of the growing efficiencies of the modern military hospital in France was food delivery. His fondness for eating had no interruptions, and whatever lingering irritations he suffered from the gas did not inhibit his appetite.

On August 9, shortly after he arrived, he wrote:

This is a splendid hospital and well equipped and they take good care of you. The food is plentiful and well cooked and very tasty.

He continued the theme on August 12.

Dearest Mother o' mine,

Just another wee chat with you. I am just fine as could be, except that I ate a little too much for dinner. Things are as usual around here.

In the same letter, I saw a reference that once again brought my search for my grandfather—the project I had assigned myself when we found his letters—eerily back into perspective. He enclosed a copy of *The Stars and Stripes* that detailed the death of Billy Schupp—the one that had sent me on my journey. Was it the same copy? My grandfather had cut it out and sent it. He had folded it and touched it and sent it to his mother. Was that the same clipping I now had sitting in front of me?

I sat silently as I held the clipping again.

> *I am enclosing two clippings out of the last number of the Stars & Stripes. It is a good article about my job. I have been a Battalion runner since last February or so. You will note that it speaks of two Bluffs' boys. You have probably known for some time of Shupp's death.*

It is clear as August wore on that my grandfather was growing bored. One can safely assume he was feeling better because he makes no mention of his lungs or eyes.

On August 18, he offered this.

> *I have just returned to the ward after attending Mass. Everything is just the same around here, most of the time being spent in reading, arguing or playing cards, except when we are working on the Mess. Our gang, which I have mentioned to you before, has charge of the Ward Mess, that is the feeding of the patients unable to go to the Mess Hall for their meals. We draw the food, distribute it, gather up the dishes, take them over and get them washed and then clean up our kitchen and we are finished for that meal. The above occurs three times a day.*

> *Incidentally, of course, we eat ourselves and believe me, we eat when we feel good.*
>
> *Well Mother it is terribly hard to write a letter of any length or interest when it is the same day in and day out, when I don't receive any mail.*

On August 26 the routine was much the same. He was approaching his 22nd birthday. It had been a year since he had written from Camp Dodge on his 21st birthday and asked his mother, "Does it seem like 21 years ago since I was born or does it seem longer?"

At the time he was about to leave Iowa and head for Camp Mills. It must have seemed to him, sitting in Savenay, a million years before.

> *Well Mother dear, a few more days and your son will be 22 years of age. Does it seem that long or longer? Mother it seems that I have been away from the good ole' USA about two or three years already. I must write Tot on her birthday and tell her I have not forgotten her.*
>
> *Now I have not forgotten you or anything like that, just been busy doing nothing. This is such an exciting life doing nothing and becomes quite a task.*

John DeWitt did not realize it at the time, but being in a hospital, bored or not, was the best situation any soldier in France could embrace. Another enemy was afoot, one that would kill more soldiers than combat itself.

The Spanish flu was beginning to insert its deadly ways into daily life in Europe.

TWENTY-FIVE

EVER SO BRIEFLY after he was wounded, my grandfather opened up in his letters home. He seemed more philosophical, more willing to write about the darker side of his life in the trenches—the danger and the possibility of his own death. In a year's worth of letters to his mother from Camp Dodge, Camp Mills, crossing the Atlantic and marching through France, he kept things simple, entertaining, and wholesome.

Coming close to being blown to Kingdom Come and suffering from the effects of breathing phosgene gas can do that to a person, I suppose.

After he was wounded, I sensed in my grandfather a growing introspection about what he had been through and an urgency to tell his mother and father about it.

So sudden was the spate of honest descriptions of what was going on, I began to hope for more of his honesty. Briefly, it seemed to me Moses parting the Red Sea. But his introspection abated as quickly as it had opened.

It was not until he later wrote a jarring letter to his father—the first time in more than a year of letters he had written directly to his father—that I understood. That letter would come later and would allow me to understand John DeWitt's motivations more than anything I had learned in my year-long search.

His October 1918 letters from Base Hospital #8 in Savenay did not mention even in passing, the lethal and frightening Spanish influenza epidemic that was rampaging across Europe and the United States, including Iowa. I have to assume his mother had made no mention of the deadly virus in her letters either, or it would have elicited at least a comment or two from her son—especially given the frail health of John DeWitt's father, which would have made him particularly vulnerable to the flu that was killing thousands.

Old habits die hard, I suppose. Mother and son had returned to their unstated rule to not mention the unmentionable. When he was fighting, my grandfather rarely mentioned death or gas or the dangers involved with his trench-running. Once he was safely in the hospital in Savenay, where he would remain through the Fall of 1918, he never mentioned the Spanish flu.

As it turned out, John DeWitt's remarkable run of good luck had engaged itself again. There was no better place to be during an epidemic than a hospital, where his biggest problems continued to be boredom and lack of mail. In Savenay, having seen far too many deaths by then, John Dewitt must have known he would survive the war. He was not worried about the Spanish flu.

Troops at Camp Dodge did not have that luxury. If he was longing for home in October 1918, John DeWitt certainly would have been hedging his bets. Iowa was not the best place to be that month.

My grandfather should have been relieved he was not heading home. Highly contagious, the Spanish influenza of 1918 would become the worst epidemic in American history.

On October 10, 1918, an ominous headline in *The Des Moines Register,* announced a new peril:

DES MOINES GOES UNDER QUARANTINE TODAY

Spanish influenza was spreading across the country and would quickly reach epidemic proportions. It would kill 195,000 Americans in October alone. By the time it abated, the Spanish flu would kill some 20 million people worldwide.

In Iowa, schools and theaters were closed, residents began wearing masks for protection and were asked to practice "social distancing," a term that would insert itself again 100 years later. The city's board of health voted to close all churches, schools, and any establishment where large numbers of residents could congregate—dance halls, skating rinks, outdoor sporting venues, consignment stores, and improperly ventilated shops. Other places of public amusement were limited to half of their seating capacity.

At Camp Dodge, with so many men living in close quarters, 3,000 soldiers were stricken, and the camp was placed under quarantine. In one 12-hour period on October 8, 996 new cases were identified at the camp. More than 10,000 soldiers at Camp Dodge were stricken and just over 700 would die. The flu spread so quickly that camp officials were unprepared to deal with the bodies of the deceased. It was reported that the odor of rotting corpses wafted over the camp for days.

The effects of the Spanish flu were horrific. A victim would turn "huckleberry," a bluish purple. Pneumonia blocked oxygen absorption, lungs filled with blood. During autopsies the lungs sank like stones when placed in water.

At the beginning of 1918 life expectancy for Americans was 54 years for women, 48 for men. By the end of the year that life expectancy had dropped by 12 years for both.

Some people thought the virus was released by Germany from U-boats. Some said it was slipped into aspirin tablets made by Bayer, a German company. Before it subsided, one in every four Americans had suffered from its high fever and aches. An estimated 675,000 Americans died of influenza, ten times as many as in the world war. Of the U.S. soldiers who died in Europe half of them—43,000—died from the Spanish flu.

Places where large numbers of people worked or lived closely together were especially vulnerable. At the University of Iowa in Iowa City, 38 staff and students died. Anyone entering or leaving the campus had to show a pass, which was checked by military police called in for the emergency. Iowa State College in Ames, where 52 would die, passes were also required. After its campus hospital filled to capacity with flu victims, the sick were housed in the gym.

The 1918 strain of the virus that wreaked havoc on the troops in Europe actually started in Kansas, when a doctor in the southwest corner of the state described a particularly virulent strain in the year's first influenza cases in January and February 1918.

At Camp Funston, in eastern Kansas, a large induction and training center of more than 50,000 soldiers, there were hundreds of cases of this new strain by March. It was first identified at Fort Riley, Kansas, when a private named Albert Gitchell checked himself into the base hospital complaining of a sore throat, fever, and headache. Soon after one hundred more Fort Riley soldiers had done the same.

By summer, soldiers who had trained at bases like Fort Riley, Camp Funston, and Camp Dodge would be arriving in Europe to fight.

The Spanish flu would hit France in April, accompanying and spreading among the tightly packed men aboard transports heading to Europe. In September through November 1918, influenza and pneumonia sickened twenty to forty percent of U.S. Army and Navy personnel.

Base hospitals, included Base Hospital #8 in Savenay, were prepared for the onslaught, setting up new influenza wards and providing excellent nursing care. Most influenza deaths were caused by complications from pneumonia, for which there was no antibiotics in 1918.

Nursing care, then, involved isolating patients and offering palliative measures only. One base hospital nurse described her job:

> *Our chief duties were to give medicines to the patients, fix ice packs, feed them at [meal] time, rub their back or chest with camphorated sweet oil, [and] make egg-nogs.*

Another nurse recalled her surprise at how rapidly conditions deteriorated.

> *We didn't have time to treat them. We didn't take temperatures; we didn't even have time to take blood pressures. There was a man lying on the bed dying and one was lying on the floor. Another man was on a stretcher waiting for the fellow on the bed to die. Orderlies carried the dead soldiers out on stretchers at the rate of two every three hours.*

The DeWitts were blessed. John in France and his parents and sisters in Council Bluffs escaped the devastation.

I have no doubt he was happy to be safely ensconced at the hospital and not finishing his days in the army at Camp Dodge, but he again would not say anything about it.

My grandfather apparently could not escape the boredom, however. The tedious daily life at Base Hospital #8 allowed him, apparently, to dedicate himself to his favorite pastime, eating.

On October 3, he wrote:

> *How time does fly. I don't have very much to do but it seems I can't find time to do anything. Everything is just about the same. I feel fine and I am fatter now than I ever was before.*

He found time to humor his sister with a short note on a postcard the next day.

> *Dear Toad,*
>
> *Don't grow so big that I won't know you when I return.*
>
> *Lots of love and kisses to you Clare.*

On October 11 he alluded to a rating he had that perhaps had given him some status.

> *I feel fine and I am fatter now than I have ever been before in my life. I don't know how long I will be here. I have been marked in B class, which means three to six months behind the lines. This is a soft life back here, plenty to eat, good bed to sleep in, nothing to worry about and not much work to do. Pretty soft I call it but after what we went through and six straight months at the front, except the time spent in moving from one front to another, I think in a way I deserve a rest.*

You do deserve a rest, Grampa, I thought. You've done enough. Enjoy your growing waistline.

TWENTY-SIX

THE ARMISTICE ENDING more than four years of horrific fighting after millions of deaths—one of which could have easily been John Dewitt's—was signed by officials from Germany, France, the United States and Britain at 11 AM on November 11, 1918 in a railway car in Compagnie, France.

It was timed to go into effect on "the eleventh hour of the eleventh day of the eleventh month."

There were many unresolved issues between the warring parties, however, and while fighting would on paper officially cease, soldiers would continue to die.

On November 11 there were nearly 11,000 soldiers killed, wounded, or listed as missing in action, including more than 3,500 Americans.

The much-touted Treaty of Versailles would not be ratified by all parties until January 10, 1920.

John Ryder DeWitt, still languishing at Base Hospital #8 in Savenay, had unresolved issues of his own. Surrounded by the confusion, champing at the bit and biding his time until he could start the long trip home, I imagine my grandfather was pensive, perhaps a bit impatient to get out and put the war and France behind him.

On November 24 he broke a tradition he had maintained since he wrote his first letter home from Camp Dodge eighteen months earlier.

He wrote directly to his father.

For me, having followed my grandfather's path, learning as much as I could about what he had gone through, that letter to his father was the Rosetta Stone—it provided the answer to everything I had been trying to figure out about his motivations.

It took my breath away.

My grandfather and his father were obviously close. His letters home, always addressed to his mother, never failed to mention his father, to ask after his failing health, and to always offer assurance to his parents and sisters that all was well.

Shortly after arriving in France with the 168th in December 1917, my grandfather would write his mother what would be his continuing mantra:

> *Do not worry about me because I know of old that I will make it out alright so don't worry for one little minute as I still wear that smile. I am feeling fine and in good health*

He provided a clue about his relationship with his father in that same note.

> *Tell Dad that I will be able to swap yarn for yarn when I get back.*

The talk of war and killing, the stories of what he had gone through, were not for letters to his mother and young sisters. Those stories would be only between father and son, in private, man to man.

In December 1917, when he wrote that comment, my grandfather had not yet seen his friends blown to bits. He had not yet run a vital message under intense fire or taken part in the macabre daily lottery among runners to see which of them would be called on to run the gauntlet of shells and sniper fire.

In December 1917, he had not yet become inured to death as he was by the time he faced his own death in the combat building up to his gassing and shrapnel injuries.

Whatever "yarns" he promised in December to swap with his father when he returned to Council Bluffs would have been confined to the boys-being-boys stories of the barracks hijinks he'd experienced before combat. In December, he was not fluent in the language of war, death, futility, and the wrenching terror he would experience firsthand after he began running messages in April.

As stoic as he was, both in his letters home and in real life, the war would have affected him deeply.

Sitting in base Hospital #8 in Savenay in November, the armistice that promised peace signed, I suspect John DeWitt took stock of what he had been through.

He opened up to his father in a way he had not done in any letter home.

I thought of their relationship. I imagine it was not unlike that between any hardworking man and his son in a large family. I have no doubt there was a deep affection and respect between father and son, but I doubt there were hugs my family enjoys today.

There was no time for such things. Neither were there introspective father-to-son talks. In a family with no money and constant scraping to get by, there was simply no time for the luxury of sentimentality. There was love between them for sure. That emerges from every letter my grandfather wrote home. He loved his mother and father and sisters deeply.

There was the matter, too, of my grandfather's brothers, all of whom died in childhood, long before my grandfather enlisted to go to war.

Did his father wonder why my grandfather would do such a thing as enlist in the army?

Had he asked my grandfather not to?

I don't know.

In November 1918, sitting in Base Hospital #8, my grandfather knew his father's health was frail. The elder DeWitt would die in July 1920, an indication that my grandfather's concerns and worries were legitimate.

The only letter my grandfather would write directly to his father provided the answer—perhaps as a way to explain why he, the only surviving son of a hard working railway brakeman in poor health, would simply pick up, leave home, and enlist in the army to go to war 4,000 miles from Council Bluffs.

That late November letter was the most open, honest, revealing, proud, heartfelt, and gut-wrenching letter of any of the more than eighty letters he wrote home.

Was it because he was addressing his own frail father? Because there were no more censors to filter comments? Or was it because the deep emotion my grandfather had been burying for nearly eighteen months finally broke?

I believe it was a combination of all those factors.

Courage is not the absence of fear, but rather the strength to ignore fear and move into the fray. That was how John DeWitt moved through life, certainly during the war but after as well.

John Ryder DeWitt was never deterred by anything in is life, before or after the war.

That was how he lived. And that was the modest, unflappable man I knew as a young boy.

In asking his mother to be sure to tell his father he'd talk with him about his experiences, he was hiding the fact that he was bursting with pride about what he was doing and how he was excelling in the army. Being chosen as a trench runner was no small feat. The men selected for that dangerous job were exceptional in every way. They stood out, not only for their physical and mental acuity, but also for their bravery. They knew they stood a very good chance of not making it home.

John Dewitt was no coward. Being the modest man he was, he would only hint at it in his letters home.

But he was a driven young man. He was not afraid of anything the war offered. He had faced the worst of anything the war could throw his way, and he had not shied away from it.

He wanted his father to know that.

At Camp Mills he had written with disdain about the slackers and the rumor mongers who were constantly looking for a way out.

He had no time for the men who lacked commitment and courage.

The sole surviving son wanted to be sure his ailing father knew that he had done well.

Before he had left home, my grandfather was still in many ways a boy, untested and unsure about himself. The year had changed him. He had emerged as man who had seen much death and violence and unholy chaos and he had not flinched.

John Dewitt, stoic and modest, needed to tell his father he had reason to be proud of his only surviving son.

Among the letters my sister and I found in our Uncle Jack's garage, was a clipping my grandfather had sent home.

It was from a company commander to the father of one of his fellow trench runners.

It was prefaced with a heading:

> ***How Al Wallraff, member of the Company L, met his death while acting as a Battalion Runner in the attack on St. Mihiel, Salient.***
>
> *To: JJ Wallraff, Al's father*
> *At Mankato, Minnesota*
>
> *Al was acting as a Battalion Runner in the attack on St. Mihiel, Salient, September 12, 1918. Major Brewer was wounded and leading the field. He sent Al to notify Captain Lainson.*
>
> *He was in command of the Battalion and to guide the Captain to the post of command. Al found Captain Lainson, delivered the message and they were going back to Battalion Headquarters. Al seemed to be aware that his time had come. He said nothing about it. By his expressions and actions, he appeared to be looking for something to happen.*
>
> *He proved himself to be among the bravest of the brave by forcing himself on, even though he felt the hand of death approaching. They had stopped in a shell hole for a rest and shelter and were just resuming their trip when Al was shot through the stomach with a machine gun bullet.*
>
> *He died in the field almost immediately and was buried close to where he fell, northwest of Flirui, Department of the Meuse.*
>
> *His grave will always be tenderly cared for by our allies, the French.*

I imagine that was on my grandfather's his mind when he wrote his father.

November 24, 1918
Savonay
Base Hospital #8

Dear old Dad o' mine,

Well Dad, I don't suppose this surprised you very much, after all the publicity concerning Dads' letters. I know you are not much of a hand at writing letters but hope you have written me.

Somehow Dad, we men folks do not write or speak all we feel. I know that you think of me every day, Dad, and long for my return. I know you must miss me.

How do I know? Well because I think of you every day and miss you.

Out of all the pictures I received in that big bunch of mail I got not long ago, the best one of all was the picture of "Dad and Mother" and the picture of Dad in the garden. That is the stuff to give the troops. Remember how I used to hate to work in the garden? While I will still hate it, chances are, but I wouldn't mind being there where I could give it a once over.

Mother tells me how you are and what you do in every letter. Still making the schedule on time, same as usual. That's the old pep.

Well Dad, the only war we have had for a long time is over and what a relief it is to everyone. The American people were probably a joyous crew when the knowledge of the signing of the Armistice was made known. One cannot imagine the joy, the happiness, the unfettered feeling of the French people after four long years of this hellish war and at times it took a real optimist to see anything but failure in the future.

How the church bells did ring and peel out the good tidings. The people went wild with joy. It sure made a fellow feel queer to see the tears of happiness streaming down the cheeks of the old French people.

The priest at Mass this morning gave a wonderful sermon on the coming of peace and the part the Americans played. He told what the coming of first Americans meant to the French. They came at a time when the future held nothing but disaster and failure but with the coming of the Americans, was like the sunlight breaking through the thunderclouds. It gave them new courage and a new heart to face the foe with.

Dad, it sure means a lot to me to know that I was one of the first bunches over here, that I am one of the original members of the 42nd Division, a real fighting Outfit, as anyone knows. Dad, your son, who you so willingly gave, has seen a lot of action but will wait until I get back to tell you of them. He never failed to do as ordered and went ahead at all times. It takes real courage, let me tell you, and I know now that I am not yellow but at times a fellow doubts it.

Now that the war is over, I am ready to go back anytime now. In fact, the sooner the better but I think in a month or so more, I will be back in the good ole' USA.

Your loving son,
John

P. S. Will enclose a picture you can carry with you if you want to.

When my grandfather made it back to Council Bluffs, I'm certain there were hugs for his mother and sisters and even a long sustaining hug for his ailing father.

There were certainly prayers of thanksgiving and tears and joy.

There would have been laughter, because my Grampa loved laugher.

The son had returned, a different man, a wiser man.

By then he would have been hardened, not that he would ever show that side.

He was incapable of hardness. He kept that darkness to himself.

The man I knew, my gentle Grampa, was always gregarious and outgoing, and that was the side of himself he would always offer to the many friends and acquaintances he met along the way.

He came home proud of his service, knowing he had passed the test.

He would carry that with him for the rest of his life.

EPILOGUE

FOUND IN OUR Uncle Jack's (John DeWitt's son) boxes was this poem sent from France by our grandfather, John Ryder DeWitt. It was composed by little Grace Allen, fourteen-year-old daughter of Mr. and Mrs. T.F. Allen.

The Rainbow Boys

You have read the wonderful pages
Of our Rainbow Boys in France.
The names will go down through the ages
As they made the old huns dance.

How they swam the fierce Marne River
On that wonderful day in spring.
Without a thought or quiver
Of what the eve might bring.

Climbing down to the river's bank,
Swimming across to the opposite shore
Our Rainbow Boys in khaki worked
Hard as they never worked before.

Hard press ran the huns ahead
With our Rainbows close in the rear.
Huns discarding their boots as they fled,
All trembling with abject fear.

Hats off to the Rainbow Division,
Three cheers to our boys in brown
We've all reached the same decision,
Their names will all reign with renown.

And now the peace bells are ringing
Although lost his crown so they say
Thank God keeps the tune singing,
Our boys will be back some day.

And with a glad cheer we will greet them,
Those precious boys in brown
With a grand welcome we will meet them
When they land in this ole' town.

ACKNOWLEDGEMENTS

I'd like to thank my sister Abby Clutter for her dedication to assisting the older members of our family. If she had not been helping Jack DeWitt clean out his garage this material might still be in a box—in a landfill.

Many thanks to Rachel Cone-Gorham for directing me in the marketing phase of this book so I can get it to as many interested people as possible.

My great appreciation to Harley Patrick and Hellgate Press for taking a chance on publishing a book from a retired Orthopaedic surgeon with little writing experience.

But most of all I'd like to thank Tom McCarthy for his tireless and invaluable help in crafting a compelling story around these letters. His assistance and encouragement kept this book moving forward.

ABOUT THE AUTHOR

JOHN CHASE is an orthopaedic surgeon who retired in 2020. After growing up and going to school in Iowa he moved to Florida for residency and practiced for thirty-five years in Orlando.

Today, John is thoroughly enjoying retirement—spending time with his five grandchildren, playing golf and pickleball, and mentoring high school students with aspirations toward careers in medicine through Elevate Orlando. He and his wife Marian have three daughters with families in Orlando, Austin, and Atlanta.

John is also the author a memoir titled *You What?!* Writing has turned into an unexpected avocation, and he values the connections he's made with a wide array of people through his writing.

www.hellgatepress.com

Made in the USA
Coppell, TX
27 March 2025

47618205R00154